DECISION-MAKING IN POVERTY PROGRAMS

Decision-Making
in Poverty Programs

CASE STUDIES FROM
YOUTH-WORK AGENCIES

Melvin Herman and Michael Munk

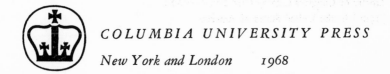

COLUMBIA UNIVERSITY PRESS

New York and London   1968

Melvin Herman is Professor of Social Work at the Graduate School of Social Work at New York University. Michael Munk is Research Scientist at the Graduate School of Social Work at New York University.

ꙮꙮ *Preface*

This collection of case studies of administrative and operational decision-making in poverty programs was prepared in response to a phenomenon that plagues any new field of professional activity as it undergoes a period of rapid expansion—the lack of teaching material based on accumulated experience. With the establishment of federal programs designed to reduce the relatively high levels of poverty in the nation, inevitably a large number of untrained and inexperienced persons had to be recruited to plan, administer, and operate them. But, perhaps because priority has been given to launching such programs and to achieving visible results in a short period of time, the acquisition of material suitable for training persons entering this field or for improving their skills through in-service training has clearly lagged behind.

In an effort to meet the need for such teaching material in a form that might also interest the general reader, the authors decided that the case study technique would be one appropriate methodology. Applied to the area of planning and operation of anti-poverty programs, case studies perform the dual function of introducing readers to some of the actual programs and procedures in the field and of illuminating the major issues that arise as personnel in poverty programs attempt to cope with some of the more typical problems confronting them.

Case studies (or case histories) are, of course, a well-established teaching technique as well as a form of scholarship, and have been used extensively in such fields as business and public administration, social work, law, political science, and sociology. For teaching and training purposes, their greatest advantage lies in their "real life" description of bureaucratic, legislative, and social behavior against a background of actual organizations, activities, and events in the various fields. The critical assumption underlying the use of case studies is that the student will be able to draw broader conclusions from his analysis of an individual case, and that, if presented with a successfully selected group of cases, he should come away with an introduction to the dimensions of his field of interest. In cases selected for their value in illuminating critical issues requiring decision-making—rather than the process of decision-making itself—the detailed description of actual events is of secondary importance to the clarity with which they reveal the basic ingredients of the specific problems and general issues confronted.

It is our belief that the case studies in this book provide an introduction to the conduct and administration of anti-poverty programs at the community level. Because they are drawn from the actual experience of personnel in the field who typically implement federally designed programs, the cases should also provide some familiarity with and specific information about the types of programs, agencies, and strategies encountered in the anti-poverty field.

As suggested above, the rapid expansion of anti-poverty programs produced an impact on thousands of communities across the country, but relatively little of this experience has been recorded in forms suitable for teaching purposes. To our knowledge no previous efforts have been made to translate it into a collection of case studies designed to identify the major problems and issues that have arisen during the first several years of operation of anti-poverty programs.

The case studies are drawn almost exclusively from the experience of programs directed toward unemployed and disadvantaged youth. Federal anti-poverty programs, of course, provide a far broader range of services, but we believe that their planning and operational problems have not been significantly different from those contained in case studies selected from youth-work programs. And although the Community Action components of anti-poverty programs include educational programs for younger children, health and legal services for poor families, and programs designed for specific groups such as Indians and migrant farm workers, the recent development of this field reflects a priority concern with youth.

The basic anti-poverty strategy of the federal programs, as contained in the Economic Opportunity Act of 1964, provides federal funds to support local programs planned and operated by community agencies within certain federal guidelines. This structure, sometimes described as "creative federalism," was strongly influenced by the youth-work programs stimulated as early as 1961 by the President's Committee on Juvenile Delinquency. And the present emphasis on delivery of services designed to permit youth to enhance their performance in the presently structured labor market was also a clear goal of these early programs.

Another reason for illustrating the general problems encountered in the administration and operation of anti-poverty programs through the experience of community agencies serving unemployed and disadvantaged youth is that, in a fiscal sense, this is where the action is. Well over half of the funds ($568 million of $824 million) spent for Community Action Programs in fiscal 1967 by federal agencies supported programs for unemployed youth. This emphasis on reducing poverty by giving priority attention to persons making their initial entry into the labor market has been described as a strategy of "breaking the vicious cycle of poverty," although it might appear that programs directed toward youth also represented more politically attractive alternatives than, for example, national economic planning for full employment.

In any case, the "youth-work" activities suggested by anti-poverty appropriations consist primarily of local Neighborhood Youth Corps programs, which provide full- and part-time work training for disadvantaged youth. These programs received $363 million in fiscal 1967. The 123 residential training centers of the Job Corps, designed to serve more severely disadvantaged youth, received $205 million. Clearly enough, federal policy makers have selected a major aspect of their broad anti-poverty strategy from the early experience of youth programs and have subsequently favored them in the critical matter of budgetary priority.

Of the twenty case studies presented in this book, therefore, the great majority illustrate the experience of community youth-work programs (the remaining cases are drawn from the Job Corps, the federal-state employment service, and a statewide youth-work program). These community programs, operated by a variety of public and private agencies, are described with an emphasis upon their staff's confrontation with clearly identified problems and with a focus on their attempts to cope with these problems.

Because our concern is to illustrate problems and issues, the studies emphasize the impact of various influences on the decision-making process, rather than describe the processes through which decisions were reached. In addition we are aware that a sharpening of focus on a single identified problem or issue inevitably reduces attention to the cluster of lesser problems which accompany the more important one. However, we believe that the priority need for teaching materials in the anti-poverty field requires issue and problem identification first and foremost and that brevity is best suited for their presentation.

Our desire for brevity as a technique of sharpening issue identification also influenced the methodology of data collection for the case studies. We prepared the cases on the basis of information supplied by participants in the community youth-work programs and other agencies who were, in almost all cases, one of the decision-makers described in the case. In most of the studies, the information was supplied to the authors through lengthy interviews followed by a review of the draft manuscript by the informants. In others, the informants wrote a preliminary description of the events for revision by the authors, followed by a review of the manuscript by the informant.

Because of this methodology, we make no claim that the material presented in the cases comprises a complete historical account of the incidents described. Indeed, other participants in the same process may view the events from a sharply different perspective, especially if they took a different position during the decision-making process than did the informant. Because parties to a conflict most often tend to justify their actions and interpret history accordingly, we cannot maintain that the viewpoint contained in each case study is the only—or even necessarily the most objective—interpretation.

Nevertheless we believe the accuracy of issue identification is not adversely affected by the admittedly one-sided view of the cases. An issue, after all, can be identified by one party to a conflict. Analysis of the various viewpoints of participants in the decision-making process is perhaps better suited to cases that attempt to describe the process itself in great detail, just as cases designed to reveal organizational structure must contain lengthy discussion of administrative forms, job descriptions, and intra-agency relations.

In an effort to ensure as high degree of accuracy as possible, however, we have stressed to our informants the preservation of anonymity throughout this book. All background data have been carefully limited. Individuals, agencies, and communities are not named, except where especially relevant to the issue illustrated. Readers may be interested to know that the case studies have been drawn from most sections of the country, that they include large metropolitan areas, smaller cities, suburban towns, and several rural areas, and that the federal agencies represented in the cases include virtually all those providing funds to community anti-poverty programs.

We selected the specific case studies on the basis of several factors. First, the issue they illustrated had to be both significant and frequently encountered during the first several years of anti-poverty program operation. We identified well over fifty such issues through a variety of sources—our personal experience in the field in both operational and consultive capacities, and a series of field visits and conferences that permitted intensive direct contact with both local program operators and representatives of federal agencies.

The second major criterion for selection of the case studies was the sharpness with which they could illustrate a significant problem. We believe that for teaching and training purposes the illustration of some conflict within the program staff or between programs is highly desirable. The development and outcome of such conflict helps the student to understand the variety of interests and pressures with which program planners and operators must contend and directs his attention to alternative ways of coping with problems.

Once the cases were selected, the form of their presentation was designed to focus upon problem identification and coping behavior. The form adopted for the case studies in this book includes (1) a brief background that acquaints the reader with information on the general setting of the program and, where relevant, on the community in which it operated, (2) a brief identification of the problem as it originally emerged, (3) a more lengthy description of how the decision-makers dealt with this problem, and (4) the consequences of the decisions they made.

The volume is organized into four sections, each of which contain five cases. The sections correspond to four major areas in which the identified issues and problems fell—planning, operation, organizational change, and research and evaluation. In a sense, however, the third and fourth sections can also be viewed as containing problems of planning and operation, but we believe that because organizational change is recognized by many policy planners as at least a major latent goal of anti-poverty programs, the special problem of its implementation deserves particular attention. Similarly, the special research and evaluation problems, we believe, warrant particular attention from students of anti-poverty programs.

The sections and cases are intended to be used either as a unified whole or individually, depending upon the needs of the instructor, his students or trainees, or the general reader. A brief synopsis, useful primarily for rapid identification of the case, precedes each case study, and a series of discussion questions follows. An introduction to each section attempts to place the case studies in a broader perspective and to suggest some general conclusions.

Melvin Herman
Michael Munk

New York University
March, 1968

ꛤꛤ *Acknowledgments*

The case studies were selected, collected, and prepared as an integral part of the Institutes and Curriculum Development Project of the Center for Study of the Unemployed of the Graduate School of Social Work at New York University. Funds to support this project were made available by the Office of Juvenile Delinquency and Youth Development of the Department of Health, Education, and Welfare, to which we express our deep appreciation.

As noted above, data for the case studies was collected primarily from interviews with and written statements from participants in the events described, supplemented by published reports and other materials. Without exception, the informants were fully cooperative, frank, and eager to assist in the production of case studies of their experience that might enable students and trainees to better understand the problems they had confronted. These informants included: Carl R. Berg, George Brager, Harold L. Cohen, Mildred Davison, Daniel E. Dressel, Fred Errig,

Elmyria Hull, James Jones, Robert Lilienfeld, Fred Lorber, Robert W. Meyer, James C. Nolan, Robert Perlman, Francis P. Purcell, Ivan Ryan, and Alice Whipple. Without their invaluable assistance, these case studies could not have been produced.

In the initial identification of the case studies, especially fruitful suggestions were made by Bernard Russell, Ruth Maitland, and Seymour Rosenthal of the Office of Juvenile Delinquency and Youth Development; by Joseph Seiler and Charles Green of the Office of Manpower Policy, Evaluation and Reseach; by Harry Kranz of the Bureau of Employment Security; by Roslyn Kane and Daniel Schulder of the Office of Economic Opportunity; by Harold Sheppard of the Upjohn Institute for Employment Research; and by Garth Mangum and Sar Levitan of the George Washington University. Our particular thanks go to George Brager, Howard Polsky, Simon Slavin, and Frances Fox Piven of the Columbia University School of Social Work who "pretested" several of the case studies in their classes and provided valuable suggestions to enhance their teaching value.

Throughout the preparation of this work the advice and guidance of our colleagues at the Center for Study of the Unemployed, especially Stanley Sadofsky, its director, was of first importance. The cooperation of its clerical staff often went beyond the call of duty. The editorial skills of Miss Anne Knauerhase at Columbia University Press considerably improved the readability of our manuscript. And finally we are continually indebted to Dean Alex Rosen of the New York University Graduate School of Social Work for his support of the center and of this project. As authors, we are solely responsible for the form and content of this casebook and, of course, for any errors and misjudgments it may contain.

M. H.

M. M.

ꙴꙴ Contents

PROBLEMS OF OPERATION

PROBLEMS OF ORGANIZATIONAL CHANGE

PROBLEMS OF RESEARCH AND EVALUATION

⚜⚜ *Abbreviations*

CAA   Community Action Agency
CAP   Community Action Program
CAUSE   Counselor-Advisor University Summer Education
EOA   Economic Opportunity Act
ES   Employment Service
MDTA   Manpower Development and Training Act
NYC   Neighborhood Youth Corps
OEO   Office of Economic Opportunity
OJD   Office of Juvenile Delinquency and Youth Development
OJT   On-the-Job Training
OMPER   Office of Manpower Policy, Evaluation and Research (formerly
         OMAT, Office of Manpower, Automation, and Training)
YOC   Youth Opportunity Center

PROBLEMS
OF PLANNING

ஶ்ஶ் *Introduction to the Cases*

The success of any large-scale human activity, more often than not, is determined by the adequacy of its planning process. The evidence to support this observation (if in fact evidence is needed) is abundantly available in the experiences of industry, the military, and, more recently, in social welfare programs. When activities designed to meet community needs, such as child care or recreation, were of relatively small scope, planning frequently depended upon ad hoc decisions made by small groups of decision-makers who tended to be protected from public scrutiny. And while their processes of planning were frequently faulty, the consequences of their shortcomings were not so severe as became the case when federal legislation in the 1960s concerned with delinquency, poverty, education, housing, and unemployment stimulated the development of large-scale ameliorative programs in thousands of communities across the land.

Soon community leaders found themselves engaged in a complex process intended to translate federal enabling legislation into viable local programs. This process required that they establish a set of program goals, recruit key staff, develop support of other local agencies, conduct research, develop a complete operational plan, and secure necessary funds—frequently from diverse sources. All this was to be accomplished under the most severe time constraints, frequently by lay and professional personnel possessing little background or experience relevant to the issues and decisions which they now faced.

Federal agencies differed greatly in their estimation of the necessity or desirability of systematic planning. For example, grants awarded under the Juvenile Delinquency and Youth Offenses Control Act of 1961 clearly delineated between grants for planning and grants for operation. The designers of this legislation intended that prospective sponsors would take as much as twelve to eighteen months for planning, after which they would apply for operational funds. This procedure provided, in many cases, an opportunity for careful program preparation that was not evident in later programs developed and funded under the Manpower Development and Training Act of 1962, which specifically precluded grants for planning.

Apparently the designers of this legislation felt either that communities did not need to plan programs to increase the employability and employment of unemployed youth and adults or, if planning were required, that it would be supported by funds secured from other sources. It is not surprising, then, that many of these programs found themselves beset with a variety of serious problems as they moved—frequently, long before they were ready—into an operational phase.

While the possibility of planning obviously is not a guarantee of future success, its absence almost certainly is an invitation to disaster. It is somewhat reassuring, therefore, to note that subsequent legislation, such as the Economic Opportunity Act of 1964 and the Model Cities legislation of 1967, enabled and encouraged communities to undertake a planning process. In examining the experiences of agencies concerned with reducing poverty, delinquency, and unemployment, one is struck by the frequency with which the difficulties they encountered were related at least in part to inadequate planning. The cases presented in this part illustrate some of the more pervasive of these problems.

During planning, minimal data had to be secured relevant to the scope of the problem to be addressed, which implied general information on the characteristics of the target population. However, planners quickly learned that this was a formidable task. An OEO report to Congress on experiences of the Economic Opportunity Act stated:

One of the obstacles facing any program of assistance for the young is the problem of identifying those who need help. Nobody knows who they are. They drop out of sight as well as out of school. There is no community in this country which can say with certainty which of its young people who left school are unable to find or keep jobs. Statistics are based on small samples and names are not recorded.

It is self-evident that the absence of such data severely reduced the possibility that planners could design a program of proper scope or size. One striking example of these difficulties is the experience of a youth-work program in Appalachia which, after it had begun operation in 1964, learned by its failure to recruit enough youth that the 1960 census data, upon which its program was based, was hopelessly incorrect. In the four intervening years many unemployed youth had moved, often to communities hundreds of miles away.

Another very serious problem was to decide precisely the central goals of the programs being designed. Unfortunately for program planners, social problems have an awkward way of becoming intertwined. Thus while it is undoubtedly true that racial discrimination, unemployment, poverty, poor health, delinquency, poor education, and poor housing are all interrelated, it is equally true that no single program can hope to deal simultaneously with problems of such magnitude, even in a single community. Not only is each of the problems enormous in its own right, but the techniques required to solve each problem vary enormously as well. For example, programs required to help Negro college graduates find suitable employment are far different from those designed to achieve the same objective on behalf of seventeen-year-old high-school dropouts who are adjudicated delinquents. In the same way, differing kinds of recruitment and screening efforts will be required if one's program goal is to reduce the total number of all the unemployed in a community, those unemployed who fall below the poverty line, those who are young, or those who are physically handicapped.

This caution does not suggest that all these objectives are not praiseworthy, for obviously they are. Rather, it suggests that planners must decide which goal, and consequently which target group, should receive priority attention in their community and which methods will need to be emphasized. And while one may be sympathetic to the planner who is reluctant or unable to make these choices and decisions, experience clearly demonstrates that programs designed on the basis of such "nondecisions" have encountered particularly serious problems. It should be remembered that the planning process usually takes place at a time when individuals, groups, or agencies with diverse and often conflicting interests are attempting to exert influence or control over the emerging program. Finally, and perhaps most important, the planning process is critically affected by the presumed availability of funds. We must note, sadly, that it is this last factor which too often finally determines not only the character of the planning process but its outcome as well.

In the first case, the planners of a youth-work program in a racially mixed community decided, on the basis of available census data, that most of the poor youth in their target population were white. They anticipated that the number of youth to be served in the program would reflect that racial balance. However, the program, when nearly filled, was almost completely Negro. The case raises a variety of questions related to planning, particularly about the evaluation of the data upon which the program was developed. We see also how differences between board and staff about one program goal (the centrality of racial balance) affected the decisions which were subsequently made to cope with the problems of racial balance. In addition, one can examine this case from the standpoint of the adequacy of the program development process.

Additional problems which arise from the existence of differing goals within an organization are illustrated in the second case. During that agency's planning process, apparently, it was not anticipated that the simultaneous goals of reducing youthful unemployment, reducing delinquency, and reducing racial barriers in hiring would all require different program techniques to serve different groups of clients and would thereby produce conflicts among those departments of the agency committed to the achievement of one, rather than another, of these goals. As a result, we see how the organization experienced difficulty in establishing service priorities and utilizing its resources efficiently. The case also suggests that the absence of clarity about goal priorities reduced the likelihood that any subsequent program evaluation could prove useful, since it would be impossible to establish what in fact was the criterion of "success."

Some special problems associated with the planning of rural programs emerge in the third case. In sparsely populated areas, planners have consistently faced the greatest difficulties in securing reliable data describing the number, characteristics, and needs of unemployed youth. Even greater obstacles are encountered in planning programs that actually reach significant numbers of such youth. With little information about the sparse target population, it is not surprising that grave difficulties must be overcome in rural programs. This case is a good illustration not only of those factors which caused the problem but also of successful efforts to replan a program after it has moved into its operational phase.

In the fourth case we are reminded that planning is a process in which diverse community groups play a part. Within an organization there are frequently significant differences of views between boards of directors and their staffs, as well as internal differences within each of these groups. In almost every situation policy decisions flow from planning activities, and here we can clearly distinguish the differing roles played in such policy formulation by a board and its staff. These planners and policy makers operating within one agency were inevitably affected by their ties to the broader community and had to balance their decision between the presumed benefits which would accrue to both. In any event the situation described finds a staff in conflict with its board, and it raises questions not only about the consequences of such conflict but, perhaps more importantly, about how such conflict can be reduced—not for the sake of avoiding conflict but rather for safeguarding the program.

The last case is an example of one of the most pervasive problems confronting the planners of poverty programs. The lack of coordination of legislation and funding at the federal level has defied the planning efforts of most local communities. Each piece of legislation and the operating guidelines established by staffs of federal departments have not always clarified which service may or may not be funded in a local program. And in the absence of information and sometimes with conflicting advice from federal staff, program planners have developed programs and learned subsequently that needed funds would not be provided for one or more components. Here, the program planners were faced with deciding whether or not to start their program even if it lacked medical services. The reasons for starting seem clear enough, as do the consequences of this decision for the youth and the program. Perhaps this case can serve to remind us that decision-making frequently involves a choice between apparently equally unpleasant alternatives.

Coping with Racial Imbalance in a Youth-Work Program

A Neighborhood Youth Corps program was planned under the auspices of a Community Action agency, which itself was formed by a municipal government. According to available census statistics, the disadvantaged youth of the community were predominantly white. The NYC program was therefore planned on the basis of an anticipated enrollment of about ninety, of whom at least fifty were expected to be white youth. Within a month after the program began operations, however, the sponsoring committee's board of directors drew the NYC staff's attention to the fact that about 90 per cent of the youth thus far recruited for the program were Negro and that, in the board's opinion, this constituted a serious problem. The figures seemed to indicate that a majority of the community's poor youth were not being reached by the program, and the committee did not wish its activities to acquire the reputation of being "all-Negro" programs. Although the NYC staff did not view the problem with the same urgency as did the board, they made several efforts to recruit additional white youth. But none of these efforts were successful, and the directors concluded that social and cultural factors in the poor Negro and white neighborhoods prevented the achievement of the racially balanced program they had originally planned.

BACKGROUND

A youth-work program was established in a suburban city of about 80,000 located within commuting distance of a metropolitan center. The city's general affluence is reflected in its 1959 median family income of over $8,000—or $2,300 higher than the national median and almost $1,700 over the state median. But at the other end of the scale, almost 10 per cent of the city's 2,000 family units had total earnings of less than $3,000.

Of these 1,900 poor families, the great majority (1,300) are white—largely first-generation Italian immigrants. Persons of Italian birth or background comprise only 13 per cent of the city's population, but probably a majority of the city's poor. The Negro population is also about 13 per cent of the total, and the 600 poor Negro families comprised about 30 per cent of the total poor.

The white and Negro poor are concentrated in separate ghettos. About 70 per cent of the city's Negroes live in three "Black Belt" census tracts of the inner city, whereas many of the Italian poor live in two census tracts of the city's "West End."

The city's youth-work program had its roots in a Mayor's Conference on Children and Youth held in May, 1964. Attended by more than three hundred youth and community leaders, the conference recommended that a work-training program be established for school dropouts and other disadvantaged youth in the community. The city's Youth Bureau, a research and coordinating agency concerned with juvenile delinquency and other youth problems, drafted proposals for such programs, but it was only after the passage of the Economic Opportunity Act (EOA) three months later that implementation became feasible.

In October, 1964, the mayor and city council voted to establish a Community Action Program committee, to propose and operate all anti-poverty programs in the city. One of the committee's first priorities was the development of a draft proposal for a work-training program for both in-school and out-of-school youth under Title I of the EOA—the Neighborhood Youth Corps. The committee worked closely with the Youth Bureau, as well as with the superintendent of schools and his high-school administration and guidance staff, in drafting the proposal.

The formal proposal for an NYC operated by the committee was submitted to Washington in December, 1964, for approval and funding, with a proposed operational period from February, 1965, to June, 1965. But because of delays in processing by the Office of Economic Opportunity, the NYC program was not funded and operational until June 15, 1965.

IDENTIFICATION OF THE PROBLEM

At the end of July, 1965, the lay chairman of the board of directors of the committee told the committee's executive director and the NYC project coordinator to "get more whites into the program." The chairman noted that in a community where about 70 per cent of the poor are white, a youth-work program should reasonably be expected to recruit a majority of white youth if it was in fact to reflect the racial composition of poor families in the city. He recalled that the original NYC proposal, as developed by the committee, estimated that about 50 of the 88 positions in the program would be filled by white youths. But thus far, records showed that the NYC had recruited 41 Negroes and only 5 whites. The committee chairman added that the racial imbalance was a problem because of the well-known negative effects of de facto racial segregation on individual enrollees. Insofar as possible, he said, all anti-poverty programs should be integrated.

Finally, the chairman warned of the public image the NYC and other anti-poverty programs could acquire as a result of the racial imbalance and stressed that the committee must be sensitive to community opinion. He and the committee did not wish to have anti-poverty programs identified as all-Negro programs, especially because in a city where less than a third of the poor were Negroes, it was self-evident that an all-Negro program could not reach the majority of disadvantaged youth. Racial imbalance, then, was identified as a problem of major concern to the committee.

The NYC project coordinator and the committee's executive director agreed that better racial balance would be desirable. However, they pointed out that the NYC program was serving at least a portion of truly disadvantaged youth in the community, and that positions were always open for any eligible white youth who could be recruited. They also pointed out that many white youths had to be rejected for not meeting income eligibility requirements. But they told the committee's chairman of the board that they would make new efforts to recruit a larger proportion of white youth for the NYC although, as staff employees, they viewed the problem with less urgency than the committee's chairman and his board. In addition, other recruitment problems engaged most of their attention during the summer of 1965.

COPING WITH THE PROBLEM

The first in a series of relevant planning decisions was made before the formal identification of the racial imbalance problem. Crucial to the planning of the original NYC proposal in the fall of 1964 was a decision on the goals of the work-training program: Should it be designed to reduce the school dropout rate through emphasis on an in-school component, or should it concentrate on the employment needs of out-of-school, out-of-work youngsters? The committee's board of directors, together with the Youth Bureau and the superintendent of schools, determined that not more than a score of youths already out of school could be located and recruited for the NYC in the community, while on the other hand a review of public school records of the past several years showed an average of 150 dropouts a year. For these reasons, the planners decided that their program's primary objective would be to reduce the number of dropouts by providing opportunities for part-time (fifteen hours a week at $1.25 an hour) work to the potential dropouts at the high school. Since the school records indicated that about half of the 150 dropouts left school annually for regular employment or military service or because of health problems, only 70 to 75 would be available for an NYC program and would benefit from it. The original proposal, then, provided for 72 in-school assignments (47 boys, 25 girls) and 16 out-of-school assignments (12 boys, 4 girls) for a total of 88 positions.

The first NYC in-school recruiting effort was planned by a high-school guidance counselor while the proposal was being considered in Washington, although a temporary NYC project coordinator (the Youth Bureau director) had been appointed. His mission was to recruit youngsters who would be available for work on February 1, 1965, the proposed first day of NYC operations. He decided to limit his recruitment efforts to marginal students at the high school, on the basis that students in the other three "tracks"—College Prep, Business, and Vocational—already had work-training opportunities under other programs. In response to a recruiting announcement, 94 students attended a meeting on January 21 at which the NYC program was explained. A total of 50 students completed applications prior to a second meeting a week later. The potential enrollees were referred to the state employment service for vocational evaluation, conducted by an ES counselor through testing and interviews. Of the 50 youths referred, 35 subsequently appeared for interviews and were given appointments for testing. During one week in February, 31 students took the standard ES test battery and became the initial group from which NYC enrollees could be selected.

The city's personnel manager, who was responsible for locating work assignments for the NYC program in city agencies, proposed that the ES counselor make his selection of the students on the basis of their suitability for the available jobs, which were largely white-collar aide positions in various city departments, such as clerk's aide. And since the personnel manager had located only 32 immediately available jobs, he proposed that the NYC program begin with that number of enrollees and phase in the other 56 trainees as additional assignments opened up. On this basis, the ES counselor selected 24 of the 31 recruits to begin work as soon as the NYC program was funded by the OEO. This first group was evenly divided between whites and Negroes. The seven remaining youngsters, in his judgment, were not suitable for any of the 32 available jobs.

Thus, while the 24 students were available in early February and others were processed through the same procedure during the spring, the OEO's delay in approving the contract had a serious effect on further recruitment efforts. The NYC contract was not signed until May, 1965, when the committee hired its first executive director (a local Negro leader, active in the civil rights movement). In June, when the program received its first funds, most of the youths recruited during the winter and spring had lost interest and hope in the NYC. School was closing for the summer, and instead of a part-time work program for those in school, the NYC was faced with the need to provide full-time summer work for most of its potential enrollees.

The first permanent NYC project coordinator, a white clergyman with only a year's residence in the city, was hired immediately after the program was funded. Reviewing the recruiting efforts of the winter and spring, he found that de facto responsibility had been delegated to the high-school guidance counselor and the ES counselor. These planners had based their criterion for recruitment primarily on the youngsters' suitability for available work assignments, and not sufficiently on their eligibility for the NYC program according to their family income. Since the level of income had received insufficient attention in the first recruitment campaign, the new project coordinator soon discovered that several enrollees placed in work assignments were not "poor." He therefore was forced to discharge four of the twenty enrollees assigned in late June because their families had incomes over $3,000 for a family of two (plus $500 for each additional member).

This income standard for eligibility was set by the project coordinator, who revised upward the widely used but unofficial Department of Labor standard of $3,000 for a family of four. He based this decision on the committee's earlier determination that their particular community had, because of its affluence, living costs sharply higher than the national average and on the fact that the national eligibility standard was lower than the amount currently being received by many public welfare recipients in the community.

When the project coordinator established $3,000 for a family of two as his eligibility standard in late June, he immediately began to enforce the new eligibility requirements, stressing that the standard was designed to aid only the poor and disadvantaged youths in the community. The youths who had to be dismissed because their families' incomes were above the standard had been enrolled on the basis of the first recruitment campaign conducted by the school and employment service counselors.

The problem of income eligibility became major during the summer of 1965, when many youths were attracted to the NYC after word spread that it was a "place to get a summer job." The office was swamped in early July with hundreds of job-seekers, the majority of whom were well above the poverty standard set by the project coordinator. College students on vacation, high-school graduates needing funds for college entrance in the fall, and others, totaling three hundred youngsters, were turned away by the NYC during the summer.

Racial imbalance was related to the income eligibility problem since a much higher proportion of white youths were found to be "above income" for the NYC. Of the first three whites actually assigned (in the initial group of six youngsters) in mid-June, one had to be terminated when the standard of $3,000 for a family of two was applied.

In the absence of a formal directive from the federal NYC office on income eligibility, the project coordinator sought clarification of this problem at a regional conference of NYC staffs held in August, 1965. The conference concluded that local NYC directors should exercise judgment on the precise definition of poverty in their own communities, and the NYC coordinator and committee's executive director were confident that their standard was realistic. However, in September, 1965, a federal NYC program guideline which set a poverty index at $1,990 for a family of two and $3,130 for a family of four was made available to the NYC staff. The project coordinator was thus required to enforce the new guideline and again discharge some youth recruited under his previous criteria. Because he felt great responsibility for the summer recruitment and because some of the "above-income" enrollees were not yet prepared for regular employment, he retained them in the program despite the new federal directive.

Both the project coordinator and the committee's executive director believed that the federal guideline was unrealistically low for their community. (Subsequently, in November, 1966, the local council of social welfare agencies adopted a recommendation of $4,700 for a family of four as the poverty line.) At the same time, those who were eligible under the new guidelines were subjected to such a highly complex enrollment process that only the very strongly motivated were able to complete it successfully. The process involved ten separate steps, appointments, and referrals which normally took one to two weeks to complete. A missed appointment would add as much as an additional week to the process. A simplified procedure was adopted in the winter of 1965. During the entire first summer of operations, the NYC program consistently had more youth "in process" than were actually on the job. A total of 71 enrollees were placed on jobs at some time during the summer, but by September 1, 1965, only 45 were still working—little more than half the projected total of 88.

The following table shows the cumulative NYC enrollment in 1965:

	Total Enrollment to Date	Number White	Per Cent White
June 15	6	3	50
End of June	20	3	15
End of July	46	5	10
End of August	71	8	11
End of September	80	8	10
End of October	88	11	12
End of November	106	15	14
End of December	120	16	13

Attempts to cope with the problem of racial imbalance in the NYC program began informally during the summer of 1965 with a search for the causes of a 90 per cent Negro enrollment in a community where almost three-quarters of the poor were white. The staff noted that recruitment had consisted primarily of referrals from the local welfare, police, and probation departments; school agencies; the housing authority; Youth Bureau; and boys' clubs. None of these agencies served a predominantly Negro clientele. Work assignments included both white-collar and blue-collar jobs. The NYC project coordinator and most of the work supervisors in the city agencies where the enrollees worked were white.

One factor was identified as having a major influence on the racial imbalance of the NYC program—the public image of the Community Action Program as an arm of the civil rights movement. Previous to the establishment of the committee, a widely publicized effort to integrate the elementary schools in the city was conducted, and some of its leaders, including the committee's executive director, later became part of the anti-poverty agency. In addition, civil rights organizations, such as NAACP and CORE, had sent youngsters to the NYC.

It was also determined that most of the white enrollees had been referred by the welfare department and did not live in the predominantly poor white West End, whereas most of the Negro enrollees lived in the Negro ghetto. It was therefore assumed by the NYC director that communication between enrollees and others in their neighborhoods was enhanced in the Negro ghetto, but almost nonexistent in the West End. As early enrollment, in effect, reinforced the public image of the NYC (and other anti-poverty programs) as "Negro programs," the obstacles to white recruitment increased.

Another reflection of the barriers between poor Negro and white youths in the community was seen in the racial composition of participants in the Teen Center. This Teen Center was established jointly by the committee and the Youth Bureau as an experimental effort to provide disadvantaged youth with an "enrichment" program of small group activities, such as acting, painting, sewing, photography, and remedial education. A racial balance (fifty white and fifty Negro youth) was set as a goal by the Youth Bureau planners.

However, recruitment was not intensive for these small group activities, and few youngsters joined. Very few white youth participated, and those who did were largely interested in the tutorial program, not the cultural enrichment activities. When social dancing was provided on Friday and Saturday nights in the Teen Center, which was located in the committee's building in an urban renewal area, it first attracted a predominantly Negro group, and later in the summer of 1965, an exclusively Negro one. As many as three hundred Negro youth came to the weekly dances. All members of the Teen Center's board of directors, elected by the participants, were Negro NYC enrollees. Because the center also became an especially active recruitment source for the NYC, the program's all-Negro image was again reinforced.

In the fall of 1965 a specific effort was made to integrate the Teen Center by assigning several white NYC enrollees to work in the center. These youngsters soon requested transfers to what they described as "more meaningful" assignments, and the effort failed to attract white participants to the center.

The NYC project coordinator and the committee's executive director drew the following conclusions during the summer of 1965:

1. The stricter enforcement of income eligibility standards tended to eliminate more white than Negro youngsters from the NYC program, although statistics showed three times as many white families below any given "poverty line."

2. Enrollment records showed that Negro youths in the ghetto were "recruiting" in their neighborhoods by telling their friends about their jobs, but the lack of white youths from the poor white neighborhoods reduced the possibility of word-of-mouth recruitment there.

3. The all-Negro image of the community's anti-poverty programs had been reinforced by the racial composition of the NYC enrollees and the participants in the Teen Center.

4. Despite the racial imbalance, the program always had openings for several youths, white or Negro, and the staff remained convinced that it was helping at least part of the target population. The problem was, therefore, not viewed by the staff as of the greatest urgency.

All referring agencies were informed that more white youths were being sought for the program, and in the fall school guidance counselors were asked to make special efforts to help achieve a better racial balance. But enrollees continued to be referred at the prevailing 90 to

10 Negro/white ratio, and it was assumed that few if any efforts were actually made by the referring agencies with the exception of the welfare department and boys' clubs. These two agencies supplied almost all the white youth enrolled in the NYC program. Next the committee's executive director and the NYC project coordinator devoted a portion of their speaking engagements in the community to publicizing the fact that openings existed in the NYC and that they were especially eager to recruit disadvantaged white youth. The project coordinator personally asked clergymen, church groups, and boys' clubs in the Italian neighborhoods to refer white youngsters.

CONSEQUENCES

As a result of these efforts, a relatively small number of additional white youth did appear at the NYC office, but almost all were from families above the federal poverty line (by $700 to $1,000 a year) and were generally employable in better jobs than the NYC could provide. One group of youths from the Italian area, however, told a staff member that when a group of youngsters from the area had tried to enroll in the NYC, Negro boys prevented them from entering the office, telling them the program was for Negroes only. Although there was no verification of this report, it did illustrate the image of the NYC program held by some disadvantaged white youth.

The continued racial imbalance of the program resulted in two major administrative decisions in late August by the committee's executive director and the project coordinator, which were fully endorsed by the board of directors of the committee. The first was the almost total elimination of NYC enrollee meetings, which many other cities utilized each payday for films, talks, and discussions, as part of their work-orientation program. The board and staff decided against these large group meetings because they tended to provide visual evidence of the program's racial imbalance, for both the Negro and the few white enrollees, and might deter other white youths from enrolling. Although there was, of course, no method for evaluating whether the absence of group meetings had any effect on the racial composition of the NYC enrollees, the program administrators nevertheless decided that the disadvantages of such meetings outweighed their potential benefits.

Another major decision made by the committee's executive director and project coordinator was not to launch a public recruitment campaign. Although newspaper, television, and other publicity clearly was an alternative method to overcome the earlier unsuccessful recruitment efforts toward a better racial balance, they felt that the community's poor should remain as anonymous as possible to avoid public identification and embarrassment. The directors also reasoned that a public recruiting campaign would require publication of the income eligibility index to prevent repetition of the earlier swamping of the office by above-income youth. Such publicity about the income index, in turn, would identify all NYC enrollees as coming from a specific income class, a situation which the directors felt would be embarrassing to the poor in an affluent community, especially to the Negro poor.

Although some newspaper publicity was received in the early weeks of the program (photos showed both white and Negro enrollees at work), the desire to protect disadvantaged youth and concentrate on their individual needs led to the directors' decision that no public recruitment directed toward white youth should be attempted. After almost eighteen months of operation, the NYC program in the city remained about 90 per cent Negro.

QUESTIONS FOR DISCUSSION

1. Are the data cited sufficient to support the planning decision to create a racially balanced NYC program?

2. If you were the director of this NYC program, would you attempt to alter the racial balance even though better racial balance would mean that a smaller total of Negro youth would be served?

3. What could have been done prior to the beginning of the program or during operation which might have produced better racial balance?

4. What might account for the fact that the program administrators were

less concerned by the racial imbalance than the lay chairman of the board of directors?

5. Do you think the staff was correct in deciding to: (*a*) eliminate NYC enrollee meetings? (*b*) avoid a public recruitment campaign?

Divisional Conflict in a Comprehensive Agency: Deciding the Goals and Priorities

A comprehensive youth agency was established with the twin objectives of "preventing and treating" juvenile delinquency by providing youth with genuine opportunities for jobs, education, and community participation. The agency established several divisions for providing these services, among which were a work-training and placement program and a street-gang program.

The youth-work program was designed to provide job-training and placement services for all youth requiring them, and the street-gang program was to provide alternatives to antisocial behavior by gang members and other "hard-core" delinquents through the agency's youth-work services. A major conflict arose when the director of the street-gang program, citing the agency goal of "treating" delinquency, argued that delinquent youth should receive priority for the work program's services, which were then unable to provide enough training positions for all applicants. The youth-work director, citing the agency goal of "preventing" of delinquency, contended that almost all youth in the program were either delinquents or delinquency-prone, even if they were not members of street gangs.

The two directors eventually reached a compromise, but the broader problem of which agency goal should be emphasized in over-all planning was never decided wholly in favor of either "prevention" or "treatment."

BACKGROUND

An experimental agency was established in a slum area of a large city in 1962 to test several new approaches to the prevention and treatment of juvenile deliquency. Generally these approaches were based on the assumption that delinquency could be prevented and treated primarily by providing disadvantaged youth and their families with real opportunities for nondelinquent behavior, such as regular employment, better schools, and better housing. These new services were to be provided through the several major divisions of the agency, including a youth-work program to counsel and train youngsters and place them in regular employment and a "street-gang" program directed toward reducing delinquent behavior in members of gangs and individual delinquent youth. The other major divisions included education and neighborhood family services.

The street-gang program sought to offer constructive opportunities to gang members. The program staff worked with gang leaders to involve their members in social action programs (many participated in the 1963 March on Washington for Jobs and Freedom, for example) and recreation. But the program's primary "selling point" was the agency's youth-work services, which paid $1.25 an hour during training and offered the possibility of subsequent regular employment. The street-gang program staff considered its clientele relatively hard core and more likely to be delinquent. The youth-work program, however, had its own recruitment activity which concentrated largely on youth who were not gang members, and this clientele appeared to the agency's staff to be less hard core than those recruited by the street-gang program.

The agency planners assumed that youth would be recruited for the youth-work program through its own activities and through those of the street-gang program, and that the youth recruited by both of these programs would be integrated into the training and placement activities of the youth-work division. They also believed the different clientele being served by the two divisions reflected the agency's commitment to both the prevention and the treatment of juvenile delinquency.

IDENTIFICATION OF THE PROBLEM

Soon after the agency began operation, a problem of priorities arose because there were not enough training positions to meet the needs of the clientele of the youth-work and street-gang divisions. The problem revealed a conflict between the dual goals of prevention and treatment of delinquency and the failure of the agency planners to assign priority to one or the other of these goals.

The problem was first identified when the director of the street-gang program indicated to the director of the youth-work program that gang members recruited by the division's staff were being subjected to serious delays in work assignment. The gang workers complained that some of their clients had to wait so long for assignment that they were becoming disillusioned with the agency and the program and were leaving it. They were concerned that, if the program developed a reputation of subjecting youngsters to long delays, it would become increasingly difficult to recruit gang youth and that the agency's program would be in jeopardy.

The director of the youth-work program responded that because the number of youth applying for the training program was larger than anticipated there had indeed been some delays in assignments, but that this was the experience of all trainees, not only of those recruited by the gang workers. He also indicated that every effort was being made to reduce waiting periods for all youngsters.

But the street-gang director pointed out that a major goal of the agency was the treatment of youth already adjudged delinquent by providing legitimate job opportunities. If the agency were actually to provide this opportunity, the director believed, first priority for its services must be given to delinquent youth—that is, the gang members and hard-core youngsters that the street-gang program was recruiting. Further, the director pointed out, it was much more difficult to recruit the hard-core delinquents who would not normally enter the program without intensive efforts by his staff. If they were then delayed in starting their job training, they would not be so likely to return for additional appointments and future openings as would the youth who were not gang members. All these factors, the street-gang director argued, suggested that blanket priority for training positions in the agency's youth-work program routinely should go to youth recruited by the street-gang division. If the agency's resources were insufficient to serve all youth in the area, the "most damaged" must be served first.

The youth-work director, in turn, stressed the importance of the other major agency goal—the prevention of juvenile delinquency. He suggested that all the youth receiving work-training and placement services were prone to delinquent behavior since they resided in the identical social and physical environment as the gang members. Without the opportunities offered by the agency's programs, he said, they might well become delinquents themselves. Furthermore, he noted, a high proportion of the trainees were known by other trainees to be delinquent, although they did not necessarily have police records or belong to street gangs. The work program, therefore, in assigning trainees to openings on an equal basis, was in effect attempting to meet both goals of the agency. Finally, he argued, if the community felt that the youth-work program actually favored hard-core delinquents and discriminated against "ordinary poor kids," the agency's reputation in the community and its ability to operate could be adversely affected. As a matter of fact, hostility was already manifest in the community. A picket line had been established by some neighborhood youth to express resentment of the priority delinquent youth were receiving in work training and job placement. One sign read: "I can't get a job because I haven't killed anybody—yet."

The street-gang director replied that in his view some significant portion of the youth recruited by the youth-work program were in no sense delinquent or hard core. Indeed, he had observed that some training positions were filled with high-school graduates from stable family backgrounds who did not appear to need any special social services. The youth-work director agreed that some of these youth were indeed recruited by the program, but that they were mostly Negro high-school graduates undergoing special preparation as part of the agency's efforts to break down racial barriers in employment which, he pointed out, was another major goal of the agency. Nevertheless the street-gang director continued to suggest that there was some evidence of "creaming" in the program and that the agency was committed to work with the hard-core youth usually neglected by traditional social agencies.

The problem confronting the agency, therefore, was specifically whether delinquent youth should receive priority for its services, but this question also implied the need to decide which of its basic goals— the prevention or the treatment of juvenile delinquency—was to have priority in its overall program planning.

COPING WITH THE PROBLEM

A subsequent series of meetings between the directors of the street-gang and youth-work programs failed to resolve the conflict on priority treatment of delinquent youth. The street-gang director continued to insist that his clients receive priority, especially since existing service agencies in the area had traditionally avoided the hard-core youth. The youth-work director continued to stress his belief that many delinquent and delinquency-prone youth would be denied service if the gang members received priority and that the long-range solution (not feasible because of budgeting restrictions) should be expansion of the program to accommodate all youth who needed job-training and placement services.

Because the two program directors failed to reach agreement, the issue was referred to the agency administrators and by them to the executive staff committee (composed of the five division directors). It immediately became clear that the problem extended to all their divisions, because the conflict posed the question whether the families of delinquents should receive priority for housing, family, or educational services offered by the comprehensive agency. Solution to the problem seemed to call for a basic policy statement by the agency's board of directors—one that would commit the agency to work primarily either for the prevention or for the treatment of delinquency. The directors also suggested that the conflict required a decision on whether the agency should concern itself primarily with the rehabilitation of delinquents or with broader institutional change in the community as a whole.

But before these issues were resolved, the youth-work and street-gang directors reached a compromise. Encouraged both by the executive staff committee and by the agency administrators, the two directors decided that a specified number of openings for training positions would be set aside each week for youth recruited by the street-gang division. They later agreed that of the approximately sixty new openings each week the number would be ten. But the agreement did not make such a priority routine; if the gang workers were unable to fill these ten positions each week, the unfilled priority positions would be assigned to the "walk-ins" or those recruited through other means.

CONSEQUENCES

The compromise agreement reached by the youth-work and street-gang directors successfully resolved the specific conflict between the two divisions of the agency. In general the steet-gang staff filled their ten priority openings with members of the same gang and thus were able to recruit youngsters who could only be persuaded to apply together with other members of their own gang. The staff was also able to demonstrate to the hard-core youth that the agency could deliver what it promised without undue delay. At the same time there were few complaints from other youth since the great majority of new training openings were still being filled in the previous manner.

But for the agency's board of directors the clarification of goals remained a major problem. In an effort to define its commitment to prevention (institutional change) or to treatment (rehabilitation) of juvenile delinquency, the board issued a new formulation of its objectives in June, 1963, about 9 months after it had begun operation and shortly after the resolution of the conflict between the youth-work and street-gang divisions.

The new objectives reiterated the agency's commitment to both prevention and treatment of juvenile delinquency and reaffirmed that parolees, gang members, and other hard-core youth would receive preference over "other" poor youth of the community. But the agency significantly qualified this list of priorities by noting that some members of the hard-core group might require more intensive services than the rest of the target population. The board warned that the agency should not be "taken over" by clients requiring extensive rehabilitative services and therefore decided that not more than "20 to 30 per cent" of the program's clientele should require a longer period of service than the average trainee, which at that time was about six months.

For most of the executive staff committee and the agency administrators, this statement suggested a shift from the agency's original commitment to the hard-core youth of the community at the expense of the "preventive" objective. The statement seemed to imply that if priority were given to the "most damaged" clients the program's services would gradually be taken over by these groups and fewer resources would be available to the general target population.

QUESTIONS FOR DISCUSSION

1. What could have been done during the planning period that might have reduced conflict between the two programs?

2. Why do you think the board of directors was unable to arrive at a clear-cut policy statement concerning service priorities?

3. To what extent were the ensuing conflicts an inevitable result of the multiple goals of the agency?

4. Was the compromise agreement an effective way to resolve this conflict?

5. In this type of comprehensive anti-delinquency program, do you believe that priority treatment for "hard-core" youth is desirable?

Planning a Rural Youth-Work Program:
The Residential Solution

Operators of a university-based training center serving a depressed and sparsely settled rural area discovered that their training programs were not reaching the disadvantaged rural youth among the target population. In an effort to cope with this problem, they designed an intensive recruitment and referral program that was to reach 1,000 rural youth for placement in regular jobs, on-the-job or vocational training, or referral to specialized supportive services near their homes.

Soon after the project began operations, the staff concluded that the sparsely settled rural area could not provide an adequate number of full-time jobs, OJT work sites, or supportive services to meet the needs of the target population. Therefore a decision was made to provide vocational training at the university's area training center, while the youth stayed in a group residence. The project also oriented both the trainees and their families to the prospect of relocation after completion of the training. In general the residential strategy proved considerably more successful in training rural youth for employment away from their homes than did the original, more conventional approach.

BACKGROUND

In 1962 an area vocational training center was created at a university to serve a rural portion of a midwestern state, supported by funds from the Area Redevelopment Act and the Manpower Development and Training Act. Two years later the center was training about 400 unemployed or underemployed persons in thirteen vocational fields. But it was evident that the trainees were the "cream" of the unemployed

—mainly heads of stable families who were referred by local employment service offices for updating of their skills, who were prepared to
travel and establish residence near the university, and who were then
placed by the ES in regular employment as "prime job candidates."

Staff members of the center, as well as representatives of some state
and federal agencies, were troubled by the failure of the MDTA program to reach the hard-core unemployed, especially among the rural
youth of the area. A total of 27,000 persons lived in the three rural
counties served by the center, which had a population density of 8
persons per square mile (urban areas range upward from 1,000 per
square mile). The declining and seasonal nature of employment opportunities in the area (mining, lumber, and some tourism) was reflected in both the high annual average unemployment rate (over 15
per cent in 1963) and its wide range (from less than 6 per cent in the
summers to almost 33 per cent in winter). About 25 per cent of the
unemployed workers were under twenty-five years of age.

The major issue confronting the center's staff in planning the program was the difficulty of reaching isolated youth in the sparsely populated area and, once they were recruited, ensuring that they could be
referred to training, employment, or supportive services near their
homes. Even with transportation and living allowances (which most
MDTA trainees received), the younger trainees were considered ill
prepared to leave their homes and live in the city without supervision
while attending the center program.

In developing a proposal for federal funding, the center's staff decided to launch a major door-to-door recruitment campaign in the
rural areas. They believed that through intensive use of recruiter-
counselors, together with local volunteers who would meet both the
target population and their families, about 1,000 out-of-school, out-of-
work youth who were bypassed by previous programs and who did not
themselves seek out employment opportunities could be located in the
three-county area. Simultaneously the center staff would attempt to
develop sites in the area for on-the-job training and regular employment opportunities and would refer those youths believed ready to
MDTA programs at the center. In addition, the proposal would refer

rural youngsters to local service agencies for a variety of supportive services. The rural youth-work program received federal approval in June, 1964, and began operation six weeks later.

IDENTIFICATION OF THE PROBLEM

Early in the recruitment phase of the program, the directors were faced with the difficulties of serving a sparse, isolated target population inadequately provided with local employment and training opportunities, transportation, and supportive services. Through school records and door-to-door canvassing (counselors and volunteers drove more than 25,000 miles during the first several months), the names of 1,000 disadvantaged rural youth were compiled. But of these, 435 had moved from their last addresses and could not be located, 184 were females with young children, and 92 had found employment since dropping out of school. And in order to reach the remaining 400 youngsters, the service area of the program had to be expanded to include two "urban" areas—local towns with populations of 3,400 and 4,900, exceeding the Census Bureau's definition of "urban" (any "place" over 2,500).

The recruiters concluded that the long-run decline in total population of the area (8 per cent from 1920 to 1960) understated the actual out-migration of farm residents, especially farm youth. They therefore suspected that many disadvantaged rural youth had moved from farm areas to the small towns after dropping out of high school. The program staff continued to consider them rural youth despite their "urban" residence under the Census Bureau definition.

The 400 youngsters recruited by the center staff and local volunteers were, according to the planning proposal, to be served in one of four ways: (1) direct referral to local job opportunities through the ES; (2) referral to MDTA training at the area center through the ES; (3) referral to OJT at local job sites developed by the program; or (4) referral to local agencies providing physical, social, and educational supportive services. But the effects of low population density were primarily responsible for the failure of these efforts: only 32 rural youngsters were referred in the 15 months of the program's operation. Nine were placed in regular jobs, 9 in OJT, and 14 in MDTA programs (of whom less than half completed the training).

In the depressed rural area being served, the major obstacle to successful job placement was the lack of employment opportunities within commuting distance of the target population's homes. The program staff found some youngsters reluctant to leave their homes and families. Another barrier to job placement, probably found only in sparsely populated rural areas, was the reputation of the youngster or of his family with local employers. In some cases, the staff reported, "family names resulted in absolute rejection with no chance of consideration, even though the individual himself was a victim of circumstances and had some very credible virtues." The program planners considered referrals to other agencies, such as the county welfare and health departments and state vocational rehabilitation schools. Vocational schools, which were located from 250 to 600 miles away, rejected many trainees for failing to meet literacy requirements. There were, therefore, few services in the home areas of the target population.

Many of the youngsters recruited by the program expressed preference for OJT near their homes, but the staff was unable to develop more than a token number of suitable job sites in the rural area. A survey of 161 possible sites revealed 61 interested employers with 87 possible positions, but most of these were part-time, low-paying, seasonal jobs related to tourism. Training in such positions was considered undesirable by both the youngsters and the program staff. Matching sites and interested youth living within commuting distance was another major problem. Relocation or traveling over fifty miles was a frequent alternative for the rural trainees, and the low wages made relocation even less attractive. MDTA literacy screening eliminated all but fourteen youngsters from referral, and of these a majority did not complete the training program. The program staff concluded that supportive services were necessary for rural youngsters who were sent away from their homes.

It had become clear, then, to the whole rural youth-work program staff after the early months of operation, that the rural character of the area prevented the success of the planned efforts to recruit and refer disadvantaged youth and that a new strategy would have to be devised.

COPING WITH THE PROBLEM

Members of the program planning staff first suggested the establishment of separate training centers in each of the counties being served by the program. They believed that most youngsters could then receive vocational training without leaving their homes. A closer look at the budgetary problems convinced these planners, however, that separate training programs for each rural county were unfeasible. For example, the fact that training would have to be offered in a variety of occupations would require three different groups of instructors and three sets of equipment for the relatively small number of youth who would be trained. The per-capita costs of such duplication of staff and material and the anticipated difficulties of finding instructors willing to live in such isolated areas convinced the planners to reject this proposal.

They next turned to the possibility of developing a group residential program at the training center already established at the university. Some planners questioned whether they should thus encourage rural youth to leave their homes, and others predicted major disciplinary problems stemming from group residence, but eventually all agreed that, at least from an economic standpoint, the residential solution was the only viable alternative to the conventional youth-work program that had in effect failed. Some members of the staff pointed out that one advantage of a residential program would be that the possibility of the trainees' relocating to regular employment (which the planners believed was the only way they could find regular jobs) would be greater because the trainees would have to leave their homes to enter training.

Since the planned referral of trainees to jobs, training, and supportive services near their homes had failed because of the lack of opportunities within commuting distance of the target population, the decision was made to offer vocational and supportive services at the university center if the youngsters could be persuaded to leave their homes. But at the same time, it was clear from the MDTA experience that these youths were not prepared to live away from their homes without some form of supervision.

The project director therefore proposed that the trainees live together at a university dormitory while receiving training and supportive services at the area training center. In this way, he suggested, the trainees would be under supervision and thus more likely to make a successful transition to living away from home.

Another conclusion drawn from the experience of the earlier part of the program was that the rural youth trained in the residential program would also have to be placed in jobs away from home. The absence of full-time jobs paying an adequate wage dictated that efforts be made to counsel and prepare the rural youth for migration to areas where regular employment could be secured. Thus the recruiters for the residential program conveyed both to the trainees and to their families a realistic view of the trainees' prospects in the labor market.

During the 15 months of operation of the rural residential program, 120 trainees, drawn from the 400 originally recruited, were enrolled at the area training center. Among the qualifications were residence outside commuting distance of other training facilities, a willingness to enter residential training away from home, and consideration of relocation after training.

CONSEQUENCES

Involved in this decision to relocate trainees were many associated problems: Could trainees be induced to relocate? Would employers take them after referral? Where would the funds needed for relocation come from? How could the project help rural youth adjust to the complexity of urban living?

Fortunately these problems were also of considerable concern to the federal funding agencies, and funds were made available to conduct experimental mobility projects. With the help of the U.S. Department of Labor and the support of many auxiliary agencies, a relocation project was approved for all graduates of the center's MDTA programs. The project included job development and placement services, financial assistance in the form of loans, and some project supportive help at the relocation site. With the project's services and the "orientation to the world of work" sessions, most youth became receptive to relocation.

As a result 57 of the 77 graduates were relocated to jobs outside the home communities, as were 16 of 43 dropouts. Those who relocated were placed on jobs related to their training, at wages considerably higher than those who returned to their home community received. A majority of graduates returning to the home community accepted employment in occupations not related to their training. Of the 57 who relocated, 14 eventually returned to the home community, but a majority of them found employment related to their training. Employers who had rejected them previously were now willing to hire them, presumably because they had actually demonstrated their capacity to perform successfully on a job.

QUESTIONS FOR DISCUSSION

1. What factors caused the failure of the program to achieve its original goals?

2. What else could have been done during planning that might have produced a more successful initial program design?

3. From a planning standpoint, what would you consider necessary to ensure the success of the proposed residential program?

4. To what extent do you think that the problems of youth unemployment in rural areas can be solved by the encouragement of relocation?

A Community Action Program Rejects a Manpower Proposal of Its Staff

🎇 🎇

Following discussions with private and federal manpower consultants, the executive director of a local Community Action Program (CAP) and his staff proposed to operate manpower services as part of its new neighborhood service program. In the course of negotiations with existing manpower services in the community, which included the state employment service office and a newly established Youth Opportunity Center, the CAP staff became aware of great hesitancy and even opposition among the directors of these existing services to committing themselves to assist in the CAP's manpower program.

Opposition on the CAP board of directors began to develop, and the staff decided that they must secure the full backing of the existing manpower service directors if they were to secure approval from their own board. They did not succeed because of the hesitancy of the ES and YOC directors. Therefore, when the staff formally presented the manpower program to their board, they failed to secure approval. Instead, a majority of the board expressed the view that CAP agencies should not compete with established agencies for provision of manpower services but that they should concentrate on personal, advisory, and family services.

BACKGROUND

An attempt by the staff of a Community Action Program to obtain its board's approval for a comprehensive manpower program was made in a city of about 90,000 located near a major metropolitan center. The city shares many of the problems of industrial communities in its area, including a shrinking population and tax base, deterioration of its housing, and a flight of middle-class families from the city to the surrounding suburbs. The remaining population is made up primarily of blue-collar workers.

According to 1960 data the community had a median income of $6,021. Additional statistics compiled for the purpose of submitting the CAP's first request for funding indicated that 15 per cent of the families earned $3,000 or less. A recent survey of the local labor market by the state employment service (ES) found an extensive manpower shortage, with more than three hundred vacant positions at all levels of skill. The ES has also reported difficulty in filling local Manpower and Development Training Act (MDTA) vocational training positions. Statistics from a survey by the city planning board based on the 1960 census figures and the more recent survey, however, also found appreciable unemployment concentrated in areas in which the CAP focused their early programs. Responding to the planning board information, the CAP selected two neighborhoods for its first action program. These neighborhoods had unemployment rates of 6.4 per cent and 4.8 per cent.

The CAP was founded in early 1965 as a city poverty commission appointed by the mayor. It soon reorganized as a private nonprofit corporation with a corporate membership and a board of twenty-one directors. The board included municipal officials, the mayor, a city councilman, a school board member, the superintendent of schools, the director of public welfare, representatives of neighborhood organizations, and private citizens nominated from the original city poverty commission (which had as many as seventy members).

Its early programs were submitted to the Office of Economic Opportunity in April of 1965, and put into operation in June of that year. They consisted of two casework programs operated by private welfare agencies, a year-round preschool program delegated to the school board, and a Head Start program delegated to neighborhood groups. The program included a program development component but no manpower projects. Later in 1965 a manpower program in the form of a Neighborhood Youth Corps (NYC) proposal was developed by the CAP but was not funded because it reached Washington a few days after the submission deadline.

IDENTIFICATION OF THE PROBLEM

In October, 1965, two university faculty members visited the CAP to discuss program planning. As a result of this discussion, the CAP staff became increasingly aware that their program, funded at almost a quarter of a million dollars, lacked a formal manpower component. It also emerged from these discussions that on the federal level CAP's were seen as playing an active role in the planning of manpower services to the unemployed of their communities, especially where existing services were inadequate.

The CAP director believed that it would be difficult for the newly created CAP to work in the manpower field because there were a number of existing manpower services in the community. In addition to the local ES office these services included an MDTA program in operation for two years and a Youth Opportunity Center (YOC) which was gradually developing a staff and a program after a year of operation. These agencies, the director suggested, would object to competition from the local anti-poverty program. He was a professional social worker who had previously served as a staff member in the local private planning and fund-raising organization. He was well acquainted with many of the individuals serving on his board of directors and with the staff personnel of local public and private agencies. Before becoming the CAP executive director, he had served as the original chairman of the city poverty commission. He had no prior formal experience in the development or operation of manpower programs.

After visiting the local ES staff, the university faculty members concluded that existing manpower services were not reaching the disadvantaged population. Shortly thereafter, the OEO regional office representative, who had worked with the CAP executive director from the beginning of the local program, outlined to him and to the CAP president her view of future OEO funding. She predicted that the regional OEO would be very receptive to proposals for manpower programs and in fact would probably not favor proposals which did not give full recognition to local unemployment problems. She

strongly urged that the CAP develop a manpower program and repeated some of these remarks at a CAP Board meeting in November,
1965.

COPING WITH THE PROBLEM

At the end of December the director proposed to the CAP executive
committee that they utilize some of their funds allocated for consultant services to employ two members of a manpower-oriented CAP staff
in another community who had previously expressed to him their
willingness to investigate the local situation. Two members of the
board's seven-member executive committee indicated that they would
accept the recommendation of the executive director if he saw the
need for their services. Their opinion of consultants in general, however, was that "they were a waste of time." They stated further that in
their opinion the CAP had a sufficient number of projects in operation and should not expand into programs already being provided by
state agencies.

In January, 1966, one of the consultants arrived and interviewed
representatives of the following agencies: ES, YOC, Chamber of Com-
merce, Central Labor Council, School Department, and the Title V
Department of the local welfare agency. All expressed a willingness to
participate in further discussions of manpower problems in the community, although the local ES officials reserved the right to comment
in greater detail once a specific proposal had been written. Along with
these activities in the manpower area, the CAP staff had been developing proposals for multi-service centers in the two target areas. Among
the services to be offered in the centers were to be a home management project, a public health nursing service, legal services, casework
services, and neighborhood organization. These programs had been
tailored to the specific needs of the neighborhoods in which they were
to be located, and the program had been developed by and with
organizations representative of local residents.

The proposals for all but the legal services and manpower project
had been hammered out by CAP staff and neighborhood organiza-

tions in meetings of the two neighborhood groups. There was considerable interest in every aspect of these multi-service center proposals.
The legal services and the manpower project were being developed by
committees apart from the neighborhood organizations, but it was the
CAP staff's intention that both of these services would be located in
the neighborhood centers.

After evaluating the functioning of the ES, YOC, and MDTA programs (whose allocated training positions had never been filled), the
manpower consultants and the CAP staff agreed that existing community manpower services were not reaching the disadvantaged population concentrated in the target neighborhoods. They further agreed
that the employment and training needs of these residents could best
be met through services available in their neighborhoods, and that
one of the reasons why the existing manpower services failed to reach
disadvantaged persons was the remote and inconvenient locations of
the programs.

The proposed neighborhood centers, the consultants and CAP staff
agreed, would be ideal locations for CAP-sponsored manpower services. Duplication of services was not considered a problem because the
disadvantaged population was not being reached by the ES or YOC
local offices. They therefore proposed that the CAP establish a Neighborhood Employment Unit (NEU) in each of the two multi-service
centers.

The NEU's would be administered by a CAP manpower director, to
be located in the CAP central office, and be staffed by teams composed
of professional and nonprofessional personnel from the ES, the YOC,
and the welfare department. Each NEU team would be responsible
for providing neighborhood recruitment and on-site testing, vocational counseling, job placement, and follow-up services to chronically
unemployed or underemployed residents of the areas served by the
multi-service centers.

In addition to overall service to the neighborhood, the NEU team
in one of the neighborhoods would work closely with the local urban
renewal authority and offer intensive employment services to individuals scheduled for relocation. Job preparation programs for NEU applicants would include MDTA institutional skill training; on-the-job

training (OJT); Job Corps, out-of-school NYC, and Title V work-experience programs. The combined manpower staff of the multi-service centers would be responsible for developing job opportunities for those NEU applicants who successfully completed job preparation programs and for NEU applicants considered ready for immediate job placement. The proposal provided that the CAP and the OJT staff would not duplicate the job development activities of the ES and YOC regular staff. Job placement in the MDTA institutional programs and in the Job Corps would be the sole responsibility of the ES and YOC staff out-stationed in the NEU, and any and all such placements would be reported as ES/YOC placements to the federal government (the number of such placements was an important factor in their funding).

Prior to the opening of the NEUs, the CAP proposal called for the manpower director to work with the multi-service center directors, ES, YOC, and OEO-approved consultant in a design for program evaluation, and with the school and welfare departments for coordination of services.

When the completed multi-service center proposals were ready for review by the board of directors in March of 1966, the manpower proposal had been developed in outline form only. In presenting the outline, the executive director informed the board that OEO had indicated its willingness to supply additional funds for these programs and that such additional funding would in no way reduce funds previously committed to the CAP. However, the board gave little reaction to the outline of the manpower proposal because it was engaged in a controversy over how the funds already committed were to be allocated between the existing casework agency and the new multi-service centers.

In early April the OEO manpower section in Washington, at the request of the local CAP director, sent a representative to the community in an attempt to assist the manpower proposal through the final stages of the local approval process. Because of his past experience with local ES officials and board members, the CAP director insisted to the OEO representative that unequivocal public statements of support by the ES manager and YOC director (a former ES office manager) were required by the CAP board before it would endorse the proposals. The OEO representative was requested to meet again with these two individuals.

At that meeting the ES manager indicated that his operations were already severely understaffed and that he would be unable to meet any request to out-station personnel in the multi-service centers. He said, however, that the ES would do so if ordered to by superiors at the state level. The local ES manager was a young man who had recently arrived in the community and was serving on an interim basis. Although personally cooperative, he was extremely sensitive to the structure and policies of the state agency by whom he was employed. During the negotiations he frequently expressed his willingness to perform any task on behalf of the CAP or to institute any change in ES procedures if instructed to do so by his superiors. He would not assume responsibility for requesting the initiation of any such change, however.

After the OEO manpower representative had departed, the ES regional supervisor met with the CAP director. He, along with his ES local manager, softened their original stand to the point where they urged the CAP director to write to the state ES director requesting the out-stationing of ES personnel in multi-service centers. They were still unwilling, however, to initiate this correspondence themselves. The CAP director replied that he would not take that step for two reasons: he had not received authority from his board of directors to make that request of the state ES and the local ES staff would have to be much more wholehearted in its support of the out-stationing concept if the proposal were to be approved by the local board.

In May of 1966 the manpower proposal was discussed by the board of directors. The executive director pointed out that a representative of the regional office of OEO had indicated that approximately $100,000 was available to the local CAP in addition to the previously committed funds for the operation of a manpower program. Although considerable discussion was given to the manpower proposal by all members of the board, three individuals and a bloc of two to five other members had main influence on the final decision.

The first of these was the CAP president, a minister who supported

OEO-funded manpower activities both in informal discussions and at the formal board meeting. The second individual was a well-educated, articulate housewife who had a rich background of experience at the committee and board level with a number of private welfare agencies. She believed that manpower programs were a government responsibility and that CAP should avoid conflict with them. The third key member was a professional social worker with strong background in local politics as a state representative and an unsuccessful congressional candidate. His stand against the manpower project was the only major issue on which he opposed the recommendations of the CAP staff and board president.

Two separate blocs, varying from two to five individuals according to the issue, had developed a fairly consistent record of voting against proposals and ideas submitted by the staff. Their motives were traced by the CAP director primarily to the staff's discouraging a staffing proposal of a neighborhood council and refusing to fund a City Youth Commission proposal for an urban 4-H Club program. A board member with a private welfare agency background remarked, "I don't know why we have to spend federal tax dollars just because they are there to be spent." Another advised, "Let the professionals in the field of unemployment handle that problem; let's stick to fighting the War on Poverty."

The minutes of this board meeting described its formal decision in response to the CAP staff's proposal:

The Executive Director described in great detail the status of the manpower proposal. To date, negotiations with local YOC and ES representatives in consultation with an OEO manpower representative have led to an agreement to forward a letter to the ES office requesting a judgment on the allocation of additional personnel to the local units to be out-stationed in the multi-service centers. A need for additional recruitment from hard-core unemployed has been recognized by the YOC and the ES. The extent of the problem was difficult to evaluate, however, due to the lack of statistics. Federal funds are plentiful for this type of program, but early action would be necessary in order to be allocated 1966 funds. The Board did not feel convinced of the need for a manpower project based on their knowledge of the situation. There would be a need for further explanation and probably some expert testimony on the subject before action could be taken.

Although this statement did not explicitly reject a manpower component for the CAP, it was so interpreted by both the board and the staff on the basis of the preceding discussion. They interpreted the board's reference to the need for further "expert testimony" to mean that the full approval of the ES would be necessary before the board would agree to develop manpower services in its neighborhood centers. At the same time, the staff believed, the board was aware that the ES manager would not give such approval.

The de facto rejection represented a basic disagreement between the board and the staff over the CAP role vis-à-vis existing local manpower services, the ES and the YOC to reach the unemployed and underemployed among the disadvantaged groups in the community. The CAP staff held that neighborhood manpower services were required to meet those needs of the disadvantaged not met by the ES and YOC, whereas the board believed that the CAP should not "interfere" in the employment programs, regardless of how well or poorly they were performing.

CONSEQUENCES

In the year that followed, the CAP board engaged in no further discussion of a manpower program, and the staff considered it a dead issue. The community's CAP program, therefore, was still without OEO manpower services in its neighborhood centers, and in the CAP staff's opinion the need for such services still exists. ES and YOC have, however, assigned a staff member to work half a day a week at the CAP's multi-service center.

QUESTIONS FOR DISCUSSION

1. Do you agree with the CAP staff's decision to propose a new manpower program to be operated outside of the existing ES and YOC?

2. Can you suggest ways in which the eventual action of the board could have been anticipated and coped with?

3. Do you agree with the board's insistence on ES approval of any CAP manpower proposal prior to board action?

4. What do you think the board member meant by the statement: "Let the professionals in the field of unemployment handle that problem; let's stick to fighting the War on Poverty"?

5. Is the rejection of such a staff proposal by the board tantamount to a vote of "no confidence" in the director?

A Funding Delay Reduces the Effectiveness of Planned Health Services

A private community service agency requested federal funds for a demonstration youth-work program for which it planned medical and dental examinations as an integral part of the admission process. The grant proposal included a request for funds to provide these services but, when the grant was formally approved by the federal agency, the program planners were informed that none of these funds could be used to provide health services. The planners therefore had to decide whether to start program operations without the planned health component or to postpone the project until alternative sources of funds had been secured and their original program design could be implemented.

Because youth had already been recruited for the training program and cooperating state and local agencies had assigned staff and arranged their activities for an immediate starting date, the program planners decided to begin operations without the planned health services. By the time alternate sources of funds had been found, the program had been in operation for almost seven months, and numerous difficulties were encountered because of the delay in providing health services.

BACKGROUND

A private community social service agency, serving a medium-sized city, became aware in early 1964 of the absence of any local youth-work programs in the largely rural state in which it was located. In consultation and cooperation with the state employment service and the state vocational education department, the private agency developed a grant proposal for submission to the Office of Manpower, Automation, and Training (OMAT, now OMPER, the Office of Manpower Policy, Evaluation and Research) to administer and coordinate a work-training and job-placement program for about one hundred male unemployed school dropouts, seventeen to twenty-two years old, in the community.

The agency hoped to demonstrate the effectiveness of such programs specifically directed toward this target population because it believed the state agencies responsible were too burdened with a rural philosophy to initiate such programs themselves. It therefore hoped to involve these public agencies in the planning and operation of the demonstration, with the goal of encouraging their future commitments to such programs. In addition to the state agencies, the private agency planners consulted with local school boards, the health department, medical and dental societies, and other social agencies and submitted the proposal to its own board of directors, on which business, labor, and welfare representatives were dominant.

The resulting proposal called for the private agency to recruit and counsel the trainees, and refer them to the state employment service for special youth vocational training programs administered by the state vocational education department. The state employment service also provided a training subsidy to the youth and, subsequently, placement in regular employment. The private agency was to coordinate all activities of this demonstration project.

From the outset the private agency was concerned with the provision of health services for the youth in the program. It was aware that no existing community health services were available for youth over eighteen years old in the community, except for treatment of acute illness or major physical defects. The projects planners (the agency's director and its casework, health, and recreation staff) all agreed that their program would provide both medical and dental examinations as part of the admission procedure for its youth-work program, and that follow-up treatment would be provided. As a result of their previous experience in the health field, they believed that successful training and placement of the youth would be greatly enhanced if such health services were an integral part of the total work program.

In their discussion with the city health department and the county medical and dental societies prior to submission of the grant proposal, the agency planners agreed on a schedule of payments for medical and dental examinations, dental care and psychological testing services, and for glasses and hearing aids for those youth requiring them. Scheduling of group examinations was agreed on by the more than 100 doctors and dentists and the several testing agencies providing these services. The proposal for the provision of health services was included in the original application, which was submitted to OMAT in January, 1964. A total of $6,625 was requested to carry it out.

IDENTIFICATION OF THE PROBLEM

Although the agency expected that the requested funds, including those to support the health component of the program, would be received and the project would be in operation in March, OMAT funds were not approved until June of 1964. However, the U.S. Department of Labor would not approve the use of its demonstration funds to provide health services, and consequently the agency failed to receive the requested funds for this budget item. The program planners were then faced with the possibility of having to launch the youth-work program without requiring health examination as part of the admission procedure. But the planners were still convinced that health services should be provided for the youth in the program, and preferably as part of the admission process. The planners were thus confronted with the problem of deciding whether to postpone the beginning of program operations until alternative sources of funds had been found to finance the health services component, or to launch the demonstration project without these services.

COPING WITH THE PROBLEM

The decision had to be made quickly, because youth who had already been recruited were waiting to begin their work training, and the participating agencies had assigned staff and arranged their activities to accommodate the new program. The starting date had already been postponed by the delay in overall funding for almost six months since the original target date for beginning operations. In an effort to determine whether funds for the health component might be immediately available from another federal agency, the agency staff turned to the regional office of the U.S. Public Health Service. They were informed that such funding would require about one year for processing and final disbursement.

At this point, the agency staff could wait no longer and decided to launch the program without the planned health services. They concluded that any further delay would risk the loss of most of the youngsters already recruited for work training and reduce the agency's ability to attract more youth by gaining the reputation of "not delivering" promised services. It would also require renegotiation of its agreements with participating state and local public agencies, which were already prepared to begin their services in June.

Thus several weeks after receiving the operating funds for the demonstration project from OMAT, the agency began operation of the youth-work program, with no announcement that health services were not available or planned for the future. But the planners, still convinced of the value of providing disadvantaged youth with examinations and treatment necessary for their success in the labor market, decided to pursue private sources for health services funding. They therefore approached informally a local philanthropic foundation in September, 1964, and presented a formal application in November. A $1,500 grant was received the following month. But because this was insufficient to provide the services originally planned, the agency applied to another foundation for the remainder and received $5,625, also in December. At the beginning of 1965, therefore, after six months of operation, the youth-work program had adequate funds to provide health services to its trainees.

The program's staff was confronted by significant problems as a result of their inability to provide the medical examinations planned as an integral part of the admissions procedure. Immediately after agreement was reached with the local medical and dental societies and health agencies for testing services through the six separate facilities, and for subsequent doctor's examinations when needed, a meeting was called in February, 1965, to explain the new program to the trainees and the training staff. At this meeting, a majority of the trainees appeared to oppose undergoing dental examinations, and some were also indifferent or hostile to medical examinations. And by February, after seven months of operation, only 73 trainees remained in the program and were thus available for medical examinations—55 per cent of the total originally recruited.

The agency staff decided that, because health services had become available at this late stage of the training program, the medical and dental examination could not be made compulsory as they had planned in their original design. They concluded from the trainees' response at the explanatory meeting that a significant number of trainees would withdraw from further training if undergoing dental examinations was made a necessary condition for their continuation. The examinations were then made voluntary, although the staff made intensive efforts, including personal visits to the families of recalcitrant trainees, to convince them to accept the service. Further, since many of the trainees had been placed in jobs, individual negotiations had to be conducted with their employers to release them for the examinations. A great deal of coordination between the project staff and the examination centers to schedule the variety of examinations became necessary. With health services scheduled on an individual basis, rather than for large groups, examinations at the many different locations had to be scheduled independently.

CONSEQUENCES

Forty-five per cent of the original trainees had left the program before health services could be provided, and not all the remaining trainees received examinations because of their voluntary nature and the difficulties in scheduling the individual services. Twenty-five of the 73 trainees refused dental examinations or were unable to schedule them, and 23 did not receive general medical examinations. On the other hand, 80 per cent of the trainees did receive hearing and vision examinations, 76 per cent underwent psychological tests, and 64 per cent received x-ray examinations.

The results of the program did demonstrate, however, that this group of youth required comprehensive health services. Of those trainees examined, 98 per cent needed dental care, of whom 85 per cent received it; 38 per cent had visual defects and those who could be helped by glasses received them; although no tuberculosis was discovered through the x-ray exams, one youth was found to have a serious lung disease and was subsequently treated; five trainees were found having significant hearing or speech impairment; and psychiatric examination was recommended for 20 trainees (or 36 per cent of the youths tested), of whom only two received it. The project operators concluded that both the number of trainees examined and the extent of treatment provided would have been substantially increased if the services had been funded as part of the original proposal. While the seven-months delay was a serious obstacle to the effectiveness of the program, the services provided were believed to have a strong positive influence on the subsequent employment experience of the trainees.

QUESTIONS FOR DISCUSSION

1. Why did the planners feel that providing for medical exams should be such an important aspect of the program?

2. Was there anything else they could have done during the planning that would have increased the likelihood of health services funding?

3. Should the administrators have tried to delay beginning the work training until the health funding became available?

4. Do you agree with the decision to make the health examinations voluntary?

5. Should the program planners have explained during recruitment that medical examinations would be required for admission to training?

PROBLEMS

OF OPERATION

ꙮꙮ *Introduction to the Cases*

The report of a recent study of youth-work programs in ten cities across the country contains the following statement:

The funding of a work program initiated a critical transitional period from planning to action. None of the work programs studied was able satisfactorily to complete the many complex tasks required to prepare for actual program operation. In the limited time available, work programs were unable to acquire a sufficient number of training or employment alternatives; to recruit or train complete operating staffs; to establish fully effective working relationships with other community agencies; and to complete administrative procedures and plans for the flow of traffic, schedules, and other matters of internal organization. The results were frequently chaotic.*

The first operational problems were encountered as program operators attempted to develop organizational structures appropriate to the goals to be achieved. Because it was difficult to anticipate the numbers

* Melvin Herman and Stanley Sadofsky, *Youth-Work Programs: Problems of Planning and Operation* (New York University Press, 1966), p. 189.

of youth who would seek service, or the kind of service they would require, administrators frequently were unable to make sound decisions concerning, for example, the size of staff to be recruited, the skills they should possess, their deployment in various program components, and their training. It soon became apparent that there was an absolute dearth of qualified personnel and that in order to get the programs moving many persons had to be hired who brought little to the program beyond good will and a desire to reduce poverty and unemployment.

These staff problems created an even greater need to establish sound structures which could provide the organizational supports needed by such inexperienced personnel, but these rarely emerged early enough in a program's operational phase. Administrators, recognizing that they had begun operation long before they should, made the best guesses they could and prepared themselves for making a series of changes in their programs and organizational structures as their beginning operational experiences would necessitate. Consequently, the early operational phases of youth-work programs were marked not by gradual attempts to refine the programs but rather by more basic modifications designed to cope with such problems as high dropout rates, staff conflict, and the sheer inability of certain program components to provide the services that had been expected of them. This was particularly true in those aspects concerned with recruitment, intake, testing, and job development.

The sudden public visibility of programs moving from their planning to their operational phase brought greatly increased public and political pressure on program operators. As offices were opened, staff hired, people served, and publicity received, it often seemed as if now there were something tangible for groups in the community to fight over. Program operators became targets of both public and private pressures from organized community groups who wanted a "share of the action"—modifications of programs, the hiring of certain staff members, or simply quick results in coping with unemployment. Having raised expectations in the community during the planning period, program operators were now forced to meet those expectations or face the public consequences of their failures. Some administrators began to view the first year of operation as, in effect, a continuation of the planning period, or as a pilot phase for subsequent years. Although the operation of any program requires continuous modification and replanning, one cannot avoid the belief that the special circumstances surrounding the operationalizing of these programs imposed exceptionally heavy burdens upon decision-makers.

Unlike the cases in the other chapters of this volume, those illustrating problems of operation are somewhat diverse. Operational problems emerge in all components of youth-work programs and thus are less amenable to sharply defined categories than problems of planning, organizational change, and research. The following cases, then, represent a relatively small sample of the issues arising in the operational areas and only begin to introduce the reader to the wider variety that exists.

The first case illustrates problems which stemmed from the initial creation of an organizational structure designed on the one hand to achieve a high degree of statewide coordination while at the same time to provide actual program services in a number of local communities. As many operational problems arose, the program operators found that the organizational structure they created did not provide the variety of decision-making levels which were required. And we see how, in coping with this organizational problem, the operators first established an intermediate level of reorganization on their way to a more favorable solution. Although, at first glance, one might wonder why they could not immediately arrive at this more favorable solution, the case illustrates that intermediate steps were necessary, as they so frequently are in other organizations.

How program operators attempted to deal with the unfavorable results of a rather complicated intake process is described in the next case. These intake procedures were orginally planned to facilitate the enrollment of youth in appropriate training assignments. But the program design, which seemed sound during the planning period, failed in actual operation. Rather than facilitating enrollment, it appeared to increase the number of those who dropped out before work assignment. The program operators were required to diagnose the problem and decide what remedial steps could be taken. And these remedial steps had to be effected rather quickly since the intake process determined the number of youth who would enter the program and its inadequacies posed a basic threat to the program's ability to meet its goals.

The third case provides an interesting contrast with the previous one. Here the program operators also desired to facilitate the appropriate assignment of youth, but they began their program by attempting to eliminate its intake procedures almost totally and substitute a fast-moving, nonbureaucratic process which minimized extensive early screening. While the decision brought large numbers of youth into the program, this success was achieved at the cost of inefficient use of staff and perhaps inappropriate assignment of some significant number of youth. The decision-makers were thus forced to examine the nature of the "trade-off" they had made at the initiation of operations when they had opted for their "no-intake," and although they may not have been thinking in terms of cost-benefit analysis, they clearly had to weigh the relative advantages resulting from a structural change. It is interesting to note that their solution brought them back to where the program described in the second case began. These two cases illustrate the contrasting approaches taken by two programs toward the same objective—the rapid and efficient processing of youth into their programs. After encountering difficulties, one moved in the direction of a more highly structured process, the other loosened its initial procedures.

In the fourth case we observe the effort of one program to overcome the fragmentation of services to youth which frequently resulted from the growing specialization of staff functions in a large comprehensive program. During the planning period, they designed a method of assigning each youth to a vocational counselor who would be responsible for his progress through all aspects of the program. There is little doubt that this appeared to be an attractive solution to the perceived problem of fragmentation. However, the planners did not seem to be aware that most solutions exact a cost and that a solution to one problem frequently produces new ones. Soon after the program began, these new and unanticipated problems emerged, forcing the operators to make a diagnosis and design remedial steps. In this case dearly held objectives were discarded. It may be that the ability to relinquish such objectives is a primary requirement for the successful program operator, who must be free to modify his program upon new assessments.

The final case is a particularly interesting illustration of an attempt to meet and solve an operational problem directly. The problem to be overcome is one that arises much too frequently—the failure to place in jobs otherwise qualified youth who find themselves disqualified from hiring because they cannot be bonded by commercial insurance firms. Usually bonds were not provided the youth because they had arrest records. We see how program planners attempted to solve this problem by establishing substitute devices for the needed bond, only to learn, as perhaps they should have known, that there is a critical difference between the manifest and latent aspects of most problems. And their lack of awareness of this critical difference resulted in a faulty diagnosis and, inevitably, a faulty solution.

The Missing Middle: Reorganizing a State Rural Youth-Work Program

After the first several months of operation the central staff of a "temporary" statewide youth-work program discovered that they had failed to provide a middle level of decision-making authority in their organizational structure. Nonprofessional work crew leaders tended to send day-to-day operational problems to the central state office for resolution. An initial reorganization that established regional structures and decentralized decision-making authority in the work-training area but not for supportive services was found to be unsatisfactory. A second reorganization provided a middle level of decision-making for all program components and resulted in an organizational structure that provided three distinct decision-making levels: the state, the region, and the work crew.

BACKGROUND

The day after the President signed the first appropriation bill for the Economic Opportunity Act in October, 1964, the governor of a state with a population of 7 million established a state Office of Economic Opportunity. The purpose of the new state agency was twofold: to stimulate and assist the organization of local Community Action agencies (CAAs) and to operate local anti-poverty programs until these CAAs were able to do so.

Since rural CAAs were expected to be among the last created, the state agency launched a centralized rural youth-work program to provide, on a temporary demonstration basis, work training and supportive services to disadvantaged rural youth through the newly established Neighborhood Youth Corps program. The program's central staff intended that, as rural CAAs became established, the program would be gradually phased out, with the state assuming an administrative role. The program's major purpose, then, was to ensure that rural youth would not be ignored by the NYC program during this interim period.

Relying primarily on local offices of the state employment service for recruitment, a total of 325 disadvantaged rural youth were enrolled in the program's 22 work crews by mid-July. Each work crew was comprised of 12 to 17 NYC trainees who were assigned to cleanup, maintenance, and some building repair and demolition work in state parks and conservation areas. Each was led by a crew leader whose main responsibility was to transport his crew members by bus from a pickup point near their homes to the work site, and to supervise their work and conduct on the job.

By the time the initial recruitment campaign had ended in July, the crew leaders had already begun to report a dropout problem among their earliest NYC trainees. The initial recruitment campaign had attracted the most eager and most easily accessible rural youths, so that new efforts to fill vacancies in the work crews had to focus on the less motivated and more geographically isolated youth who either ignored or were ignored by the earlier recruitment drive. The recruit-

CHART I

ORIGINAL STRUCTURE (SIMPLIFIED)
(March, 1965—January, 1966)

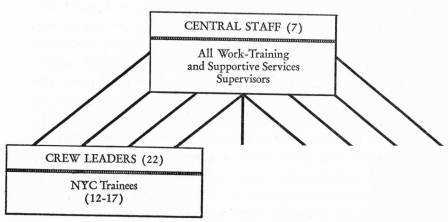

CENTRAL STAFF (7)

All Work-Training
and Supportive Services
Supervisors

CREW LEADERS (22)

NYC Trainees
(12-17)

ment problem was further complicated by the necessity to adjust bus routes to accommodate each new "fill-in" member of the work crew, and by the need to develop new work sites capable of providing more than menial conservation work that would attract more trainees and hold down dropout rates.

IDENTIFICATION OF THE PROBLEM

Coping with such recruiting, transportation, and work-site problems was originally considered to be the responsibility of the individual crew leaders (see Chart I). But increasingly the program's central staff, which was located in the state capital, received requests from crew leaders for guidance in the handling of such problems. How and where could they find eligible youth to fill vacancies in their work crews? From how far out of their established bus route could they accept new trainees? Where could they find new work sites when the work on the state parks was completed?

The central staff found that it was spending more and more of its time dealing with problems which the nonprofessional crew leaders were unable to resolve. One of the central staff, the employment serv-

ice liaison director, found that one-third of his time was being con-
sumed by travel to work sites, while waves of phone calls from worried
crew leaders engulfed the central office of the program.

Before the end of the summer of 1965, the central staff agreed that a
crucial middle level of decision-making authority (between the crew
and the statewide levels) was missing from their organizational structure. This middle level was needed to deal with operational problems
that experience indicated were too complex to be resolved by the crew
leaders but at the same time were not appropriate to the central staff.
In short, a distribution of decision-making authority that corre-
sponded to the three major functional levels of the organization—the
crew, the state, and "the middle"—was required. Only one member of
the central staff voiced any objection to this analysis of the problem:
he warned against the creation of an "unwieldy bureaucracy."

With this one exception, there was agreement among the central
staff that the middle level could best be introduced into the organizational structure of the program by dividing the state into three regions, each headed by a regional supervisor. These regional supervisors would then have responsibility for making decisions concerning
other than day-to-day intra-work crew problems (which would remain
with the crew leader) and overall policy and planning (which would
remain with the central staff). These administrative regions had already been established in effect by the initial recruitment campaign,
which was conducted separately in the southern, central and northern
regions of the state.

Although the central staff agreed on the principle of regionalization, they disagreed about the precise level and scope of decision-
making authority to be delegated to the regional supervisors. In fact
the central staff considered alternate models of the new organizational
structure for several months before the director of the state program
reached a final decision.

COPING WITH THE PROBLEM

The principal advocate of speedy regionalization was the employment service liaison director. He had proposed it even before the

absence of a middle-level decision-making authority was generally identified as a major problem because he had been most frequently called upon to assist many of the crew leaders with their problems since mid-July. Hesitancy was expressed primarily by the program director, who of course had to make the final decision on just how much authority the regional supervisors would have.

The proponents of complete and prompt regionalization argued that the regional supervisors should have authority over all middle-range decision-making in their region, including the work-training and supportive services components. Otherwise they feared authority would be split and operational problems would be compounded rather than resolved by the reorganization.

The program director on the other hand did not believe that there were experienced personnel among the present staff who could adequately supervise both the training and supportive services components of the program. He pointed out that budget limitations would seriously limit the level at which the regional supervisors could be hired and stated that in his view none of the field supervisors could assume regional authority. Discussions and memorandums among the central staff over this issue occupied the period from July to September of 1965.

In September two members of the central staff, the employment service liaison director and the assistant chief for field operations, offered to become regional supervisors themselves. They hoped this would indicate to the program director the level at which they believed these positions should be filled and also the urgency with which they viewed the need for regionalization. They argued that personnel qualified to handle all program components must be appointed to the regional posts and that a compromise on either the level of the personnel or on their functions would lead to failure of the regionalization. The liaison director felt so strongly about this issue that he threatened to resign if the reorganization was not implemented by November of 1965.

The program director rejected his assistants' suggestion that they be appointed regional supervisors because, he said, their services were required at the policy-making and planning level in the central office. But the pressure from the central staff contributed to his decision to

CHART II

FIRST REORGANIZATION (SIMPLIFIED)

(January, 1966 – September, 1966)

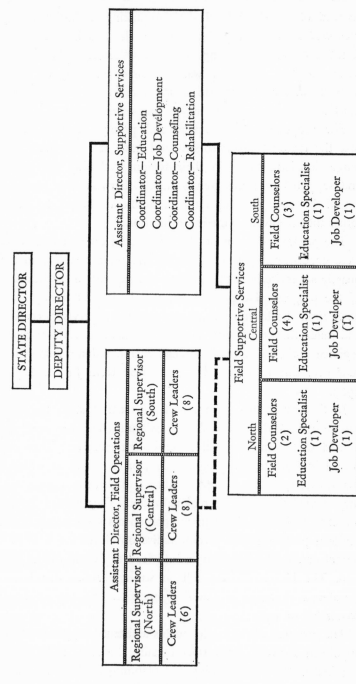

implement reorganization at that time. The program director resolved the issue by appointing the three most highly qualified crew leaders as regional supervisors but limiting their regional decision-making authority to work-training issues. Supportive services such as remedial education were to continue under the control of the central staff.

Staff members who had advocated complete regionalization continued to argue that the line functions of the regional supervisors should be clear and complete. They predicted that friction was bound to develop between the central staff at the state level who had decision-making authority over supportive services and the crew leaders whose authority extended only to work training. The program director stated that he had based his decision to implement only a partial regionalization on the need to retain professional supervision of supportive services such as education, counseling, job development, and program evaluation. The regional supervisors were experienced only in the area of work-training supervision and would not, in his opinion, be able to make decisions concerning supportive services.

Proponents of complete regionalization, while still disagreeing, accepted the program director's decision. Neighborhood Youth Corps approval for the partial regionalization was obtained, and the new regional supervisors were appointed in January, 1966, when the new organizational structure (see Chart II) was put into effect. Within a few weeks of operation, however, friction between the regional supervisors and the central staff responsible for supportive service began to develop, as the advocates of complete regionalization had predicted. The regional supervisors had authority only over the crew leaders in his region, while counselors and education and job development specialists reported directly to the assistant program director for supportive services on the state level.

The regional supervisors referred to the new structure as a "spy system," and described it as reflecting "lack of trust in our judgment" by the state staff. The assistant director for supportive services (the former employment service liaison director) attempted to reduce this friction by stressing to his staff the need for cooperation with the regional supervisors and the need to avoid "going over their heads." At the same time the regionalization had the intended effect of reduc-

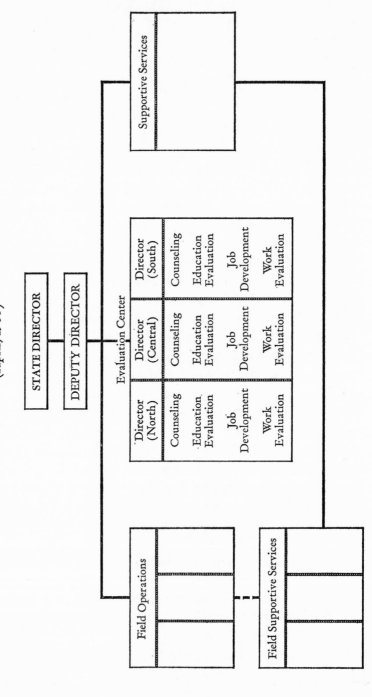

CHART III

PROPOSED ESTABLISHMENT OF EVALUATION CENTERS

(April, 1966)

STATE DIRECTOR

DEPUTY DIRECTOR

Supportive Services

Evaluation Center

Director (North)

Counseling

Education Evaluation

Job Development

Work Evaluation

Director (Central)

Counseling

Education Evaluation

Job Development

Work Evaluation

Director (South)

Counseling

Education Evaluation

Job Development

Work Evaluation

Field Operations

Field Supportive Services

ing the proportion of the central staff's time devoted to travel and decision-making on crew level decisions. The regional supervisors proved, on the whole, able to cope adequately with the day-to-day problems of their work crew leaders. They also served as channels of communication among the crews in their region.

But by April of 1966 the problems and frictions that had developed from the partial regionalization resulted in a full-scale review of the organizational structure by the central staff. The members proposed to establish rural manpower evaluation centers throughout the state for testing and assigning trainees to appropriate training and supportive services. The need for evaluation centers was quickly accepted by the central staff, but again the question arose of where the centers should be placed within the organizational structure of the total program.

At first it was recommended that the centers be created as separate agencies within each region (see Chart III), with their directors occupying an additional decision-making level. But the original advocates of complete regionalization, who now maintained an "I told you so" attitude, proposed that the centers be established concurrently with a second reorganization of the entire program. They argued that new funds for the centers could be used to hire professionals who would have middle-level decision-making authority for both the center and other program components in their region. These new structures, headed by "regional managers," would constitute the clear decentralization of authority that had been sought for almost a year.

The new organizational structure (see Chart IV) was accepted by the program director and the rest of the central staff without dissent. Its main provisions extended regional decision-making authority to the regional managers, who would in turn supervise crew leaders, counselors, and the staff of the evaluation centers. Final agreement was reached by the central staff in May, 1966. The NYC funded the proposal in the summer of 1966, and the structure was placed in operation in three regional phases from September of that year to May, 1967.

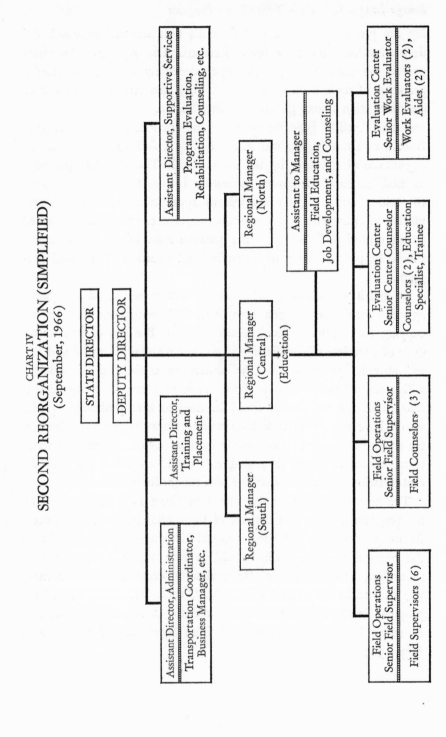

CHART IV
SECOND REORGANIZATION (SIMPLIFIED)
(September, 1966)

STATE DIRECTOR

DEPUTY DIRECTOR

Assistant Director, Supportive Services
Program Evaluation,
Rehabilitation, Counseling, etc.

Assistant Director,
Training and
Placement

Assistant Director, Administration
Transportation Coordinator,
Business Manager, etc.

Regional Manager
(North)

Regional Manager
(Central)
(Education)

Regional Manager
(South)

Assistant to Manager
Field Education,
Job Development, and Counseling

Evaluation Center
Senior Work Evaluator
Work Evaluators (2),
Aides. (2)

Evaluation Center
Senior Center Counselor
Counselors (2), Education
Specialist, Trainee

Field Operations
Senior Field Supervisor
Field Counselors· (3)

Field Operations
Senior Field Supervisor
Field Supervisors (6)

CONSEQUENCES

Experience to date indicates that the middle-level decision-making gap has been closed and that the administrative structure of the program now provides decision-making authority appropriate to the levels where operational decisions are in fact made—the crew, the region, and the state. The reorganization of the rural work-training program has had especially important consequences because, although some rural CAAs have been established in the state, the program appears to have achieved "permanent" status.

QUESTIONS FOR DISCUSSION

1. How does this case illustrate the relationship of decision-making levels to the organizational levels on which problems tend to arise?

2. Do you agree with the "compromise" made by the program director in his decision on the first reorganization?

3. To what extent can the strengthening of the temporary centralized program structure influence its transformation into a more permanent one?

4. Do you agree with the tactics used by some central staff members to force a decision on reorganization?

5. Can you suggest alternative organizational forms which might meet the needs of this program more satisfactorily?

A High Dropout Rate Forces Reorganization of a Youth-Work Program's Intake Process

The intake process planned by a municipally operated Neighborhood Youth Corps program required a rather lengthy interview and extensive testing and data collection procedures before its enrollees could

be assigned to training. In the early months of the program's operation, the NYC staff noticed a disturbingly high dropout rate between
the time of application and the completion of the intake processing.
The staff felt that the primary cause of the high dropout rate was the
excessive length of time required to complete the intake process. They
concluded that the basic solution to the problem would be to reduce
that time and enable enrollees to begin training shortly after their
first application to the program.

The NYC staff, after study of their intake process and that of other
NYC programs in their vicinity, decided that the process could be
shortened by assignment of additional personnel to processing, postponement of testing, and establishment of specific appointment times
for intake counseling. After lengthy negotiations with a Youth Opportunity Center in their vicinity, the NYC staff succeeded in having one
YOC staff member assigned to its intake program. The reorganized
intake process was considered by the staff to have been successful in
reducing the program's dropout rate, and the postponement of formal
testing until after assignment was not found to affect significantly the
appropriateness of trainee's work assignments.

BACKGROUND

A Neighborhood Youth Corps work-training program was planned
in a city with a population of approximately 80,000, under the spon-
sorship and operation of the municipal government which delegated
responsibility for basic policy guidance to an advisory committee.
This 70-member committee, which represented a broad cross section of
the community, was formed by the city council in 1952 to advise it on
problems of juvenile delinquency. A 12-member subcommittee, which
included four residents of disadvantaged neighborhoods, was selected
to act as a policy-making body for the NYC program. The committee
also established the city's NYC program and hired its staff.

Members of the advisory committee designed the original NYC
proposal, which they submitted to the Office of Economic Opportunity
in November, 1964. They provided for 80 out-of-school and 20 in-

school training positions for a six-month period. A subsequent contract shifted this proportion by raising the total number of positions to 50 in-school and 65 out-of-school. The NYC program was funded and began operations in May, 1965.

IDENTIFICATION OF THE PROBLEM

At the end of the summer of 1965, before the program had completed six months of operation, the NYC director became aware that a disturbingly high proportion of the youngsters recruited were dropping out at some point between the program's initial contact with them and their expected placement at the work site.

Since no individual records were kept of youngsters who did not complete the intake process, the high dropout rate was not discovered by reference to statistics. Rather, the NYC staff first noticed the existence of the problem when they attempted to follow up individuals they had recruited or to answer inquiries about the youth from agencies that had referred them, such as the welfare department. Toward the end of the summer it appeared that the number of dropouts during intake steadily increased. Later incomplete figures showed that 188 youths had had initial interviews by September 15, 1965, but only 88 had actually completed the intake process.

The problem was magnified by the high turnover rate of the enrollees in the NYC. The city had enjoyed a job boom since 1965, and regular jobs were available for many youngsters in the first 11 months of the program (60 per cent of enrollees found permanent jobs, 15 per cent went back to school through November, 1965) after a relatively short period of NYC work training. With large numbers of enrollees leaving the program, the NYC staff was faced with the need for large numbers of new recruits, and the problem of dropouts during the intake process was therefore more acute than if most enrollees had remained six months in work training.

The NYC director and assistant director in informal discussions with ES staff members stated their belief that the problem was due to the growing length of time required to complete the intake process.

This process, as it existed during the first six months of the program's operations, can be illustrated by a description of a typical youngster's experience.

All youth who had dropped out of local high schools during the past five years received in the mail a description of the NYC program, together with an application form (the local city school district had supplied the NYC with these names and addresses). If a youngster was interested in enrolling in the program, he was asked to attend an evening meeting held by the school district. At the meeting he filled out the application form and some time thereafter received a telephone call or a home visit from a NYC staff member asking him to report at his convenience to the local state employment service office for processing.

Arriving at the ES office (a ten-minute walk from the NYC office), he found a long line of youngsters waiting for initial interviews or regular vocational counseling, since none of them had specific appointments. Only one ES interviewer was available to counsel the youngsters, and for only several hours a day. During this initial interview, the youth was expected to decide whether or not to enroll in the program, and the counselor, through the application of very informal criteria, satisfied himself that the youngster was "poor."

Next he was presented with a packet of three NYC forms and, since these required personal and family information usually available only at home, he was told to obtain the information and return to the ES office. This normally required a second trip the following day, if the youth was fortunate enough to complete his initial interview and screening during his first visit.

After completing the NYC forms, he was scheduled to take a General Aptitude Test Battery (GATB) to measure his aptitude for job-training. Without those test results he could not be placed on a job site and begin receiving his $1.25 an hour. Often four or five days' wait (and a third trip) was required before the testing phase could be completed.

Finally, if the youth did not have a social security card, he was required to obtain one from the local field office. And if he was under eighteen, state working papers were required, for which he took a physical examination (administered by the schools), obtained a signed statement of consent from his parents, and produced his birth certificate (often a time-consuming process, especially if he was born in the rural South).

COPING WITH THE PROBLEM

The entire intake process originally required an average of three or four days, but before the end of the summer, the NYC staff found this had increased to a full week. They agreed that there was a relationship between the lengthened time required for intake processing and the growing dropout rate. They rated the "staying power" of many disadvantaged youth as very low and concluded that the long waits, trips to various offices, and complicated paper work and testing were indeed a frustrating and often disillusioning experience. Thus the NYC staff decided that a sharp decrease in time required for intake processing would be the primary means by which they would try to reduce the dropout rate of their recruits.

The NYC staff's initial review of the intake process revealed that several of its components, such as federal NYC forms and the state working papers, were beyond their immediate power to change and would have to be retained. Since initial interviewing was a relatively rapid process—once the interviews had begun—the major stumbling block appeared to be the GATB.

The staff further agreed that the major reason for the delays in the intake process was the lack of ES personnel. The one interviewer was able to devote only part of his time to NYC counseling in addition to his regular duties as an ES interviewer. To see how other programs coped with their needs for ES personnel, the NYC staff visited other NYC programs in the vicinity. They learned that these programs had received staff assistance through a Youth Opportunity Center in a nearby city and that similar assistance might be available to their program.

The NYC staff brought the problem to the attention of the policy committee in September, 1965. The meeting resulted in general agreement that the problem was essentially one of a lack of personnel for the intake process, and that additional staff time was the key to its solution. The decision was made to request the YOC for additional staff.

Later in the fall of 1965, the NYC director, the assistant director, and a policy committee member held a meeting with the director and assistant director of the nearby Youth Opportunity Center. The meeting resulted in agreement in principle that the YOC should furnish staff time to aid the local ES office in NYC processing, but also in the YOC's statement that such staff time was not now available. The YOC staff stated that whenever possible it would provide such assistance, but no specific time commitment was made.

The results of the meeting were reported to the policy committee, with the indication that the situation was becoming increasingly difficult. More and more youngsters were estimated to be dropping out during the intake process, the staff advised the committee, and the number of unfilled positions in the work-training program was growing. At this point two of the committee members who were also on the YOC's board of directors, volunteered their personal assistance in obtaining staff time from the YOC for the NYC program.

In November of 1965, a second meeting between the NYC and YOC staffs was held. Present were the same persons who attended the first meeting, joined by the counseling supervisor of the YOC and another NYC advisory committee member. At the end of this meeting, the YOC director announced that he would assign a full-time counselor to the NYC program. This staff member would be assigned to the local ES office and have responsibility for processing the federal NYC forms, testing, and job development.

The NYC staff and policy committee were gratified by this decision, especially since their original program proposals were based on the assignment of a full-time ES counselor to handle intake processing. They had been advised by the regional NYC office that their funding proposals did not have to include additional NYC staff members for this function, since they would be furnished by the ES. Since the NYC staff had subsequently learned that the local ES office was not bound by the statement of the regional NYC, they were pleased that the nearby YOC could now furnish additional staff.

Actual assignment of the full-time YOC counselor was made one month after the decision was reached. The person assigned to the NYC program brought a wealth of experience and insight into the problems of disadvantaged youth. The YOC counselor first held extensive meetings with the NYC staff to determine what steps should be taken to attack the high dropout rate during the intake process. Through informal daily contact and regular weekly meetings, it was concluded that the original problem could not be resolved merely by the addition of staff time, but that the entire intake process had to be reorganized.

Because the length of the intake process remained the major obstacle to reducing the dropout rate, in the opinion of the NYC staff and the YOC representative, its various components were thoroughly reviewed. They first decided to require definite appointments for initial counseling and screening interviews, since they had previously determined that the long waits resulting from the "stop in anytime" procedure were a discouraging factor for many disadvantaged youth. To the extent possible, appointments were scheduled for the same day that youngsters were initially approached, by phone or home visits, by the NYC staff. It was agreed that this process should not only reduce waiting periods but should also permit the YOC counselor to do a better job in the initial interview. In the absence of a group of impatient youngsters waiting in line, the counselor might be able to spend more time with each individual.

The major decision made during the reorganization of the intake process was to postpone the GATB until after the youngster began work at the work-training site. This decision was based on the assumption that the dropout rate during intake could be most sharply reduced by placing primary emphasis on the speed with which an enrollee could be put to work, in short, an emphasis on the shortest possible intake process. The testing component of this process was determined to be the most expendable.

The purpose of the tests, of course, was to assist in the assignment of the enrollee to training most suitable for his aptitudes and interests. In postponing them in the interest of rapid work placement, the NYC staff and YOC counselor agreed that there should be time for a longer initial interview during which the enrollee would talk with both a YOC and NYC counselor; that his school records and tests be consulted; and that a final conference be held with the enrollee in which his expressed interests and the suggestions of the counselors would all serve as a basis of work-site assignment.

It was further decided to schedule the GATB within a month of an enrollee's initial work assignment. If the test results clearly suggested that he had been placed in the "wrong" field (for example, in clerical work when test results showed far greater aptitude for mechanical work), a shift in assignment for the remaining five months' training could be made. It was in fact anticipated by the NYC staff and YOC counselor that many such shifts would be required, but priority was placed on getting the youths to work, not on the appropriateness of the initial work assignment.

This decision was reinforced by the NYC staff's previous experience, which had indicated that their initial counseling was most often accurate in determining an enrollee's vocational interests and aptitudes. Only in a few cases had the tests suggested different work-training assignments. It was agreed that the results of the tests could also be used for the subsequent job development and placement phases of the NYC program. In any case, the NYC staff and YOC counselor concluded that the risk of inaccurate placement was lesser than the risk of losing potential enrollees during the lengthy testing period.

CONSEQUENCES

The NYC staff, YOC counselor, and the policy committee all regard the reorganization of the NYC program's intake process as a successful effort to cope with the specific problem of the high dropout rate during intake. Again, no statistical evidence is available on the ensuing dropout rate, but all staff concerned agree that it is no longer considered a serious problem. Despite a continuing high turnover among NYC enrollees, who are still being placed in regular employment in a minimum of time (average enrollment: 3.5 months), the existence of unfilled positions in the out-of-school program (15 of the 65) is viewed by the NYC staff as resulting from the basic philosophy of moving a youngster to a permanent job as soon as he is ready and not retaining him for a full six-month period.

The reorganization of the intake process has cut the time required between initial contact to work-site assignment from eight days under the original system to one or two days for youth over eighteen, and two to four days for youngsters between sixteen and eighteen who require state working papers.

An average of about 20 minutes is now available for each interview, compared with 10 minutes under the former intake process. This is considered to reflect an advantage of the strict appointment system since it allows more time for discussions with the youngsters than was possible when others were waiting and it permits more attention to "drawing out" reticent youngsters.

The YOC counselor processes the federal NYC form (now reduced from three to one), screens recruits for eligibility under the income requirements, conducts some job counseling, and together with the youth and the NYC staff, suggests job-training assignments. More intensive counseling, as with testing, is also postponed until the enrollee is on the job, is earning pay, and has acquired some stability.

The anticipated problem of shifting work assignments after evaluation of the GATB did not arise, although a few shifts were made on the basis of that information. In general it was found that the interviews and quick placement were assigning the great majority of youngsters to the proper training areas, as was true under the old process when test results preceded assignment. In at least one case, however, the tests showed an enrollee had been placed in training on a lower level than his aptitude would have permitted. When offered an upgrading of the job site, the enrollee said he would prefer to remain in the one to which he had been originally assigned.

An additional consequence of the reorganized intake process was a new perspective on the objectives of the NYC program. The NYC staff and YOC counselor agreed that the less time an enrollee spent in job training before being placed in regular employment, the better were the objectives of the program being served. Although the resulting high turnover placed a greater burden on recruitment, it was agreed by the program operators that this problem was lessened by the reorganized intake process.

QUESTIONS FOR DISCUSSION

1. How do you evaluate the need for a highly selective and intensive intake process in a community possessing a large number of available jobs?

2. What factors other than those cited in this case might explain the high dropout rate during intake?

3. In light of the reorganization of intake, how do you assess the reluctance of the trainee cited to accept training at a level higher than his original assignment?

4. What could the NYC staff have done during planning which might have ensured the assignment of sufficient intake personnel?

5. On the basis of the problems and solutions described in this case, how would you plan an intake process for a youth-work program of this size?

An Experimental Elimination of the Intake Process Fails

In an effort to improve delivery of its services, the operators of a youth-work program decided to modify traditional bureaucratic, agency-oriented methods of operations significantly and, in effect, eliminate the screening component from their intake procedures. They decided to permit youth applying for the program's job-training and placement services to be routinely directed to the next available vocational counselor for rapid assignment (preferably on the same day) to the program's services.

But in the early weeks of operation under this unstructured intake procedure, the problems of youth requiring specialized services and the inability of counselors with specialized training and experience to utilize these in the face of a random caseload led the program operators to begin to establish a more formalized screening system.

Over a period of twelve months the operators were led, step by step, to develop a highly structured intake process as they attempted to cope with a variety of operational problems encountered along the way. Their decisions were based on their belief that the advantages of informal and rapid placement of the youngsters were far outweighed by the disadvantages to both the clients and the program. In short the experiment with the new concept of "no intake" had failed.

BACKGROUND

The operators of a large urban youth-work program were committed to experimenting with new techniques of providing social services, and they designed their procedures with emphasis placed upon meeting the perceived needs of disadvantaged youth. They therefore stressed the elimination of lengthy waiting periods, paperwork, and other effects of more traditional and highly structured methods of organization, and favored flexible, nonbureaucratic procedures.

More specifically they operated the program on the basic principle of quick delivery of services to clients because they believed that the target population's response to their program depended basically on its ability to produce rapid job-training and placement results. In addition, their budgetary limitations were such that the program's staff would have to be utilized with the greatest efficiency if the agency goal of serving large numbers of disadvantaged youth was to be met. The staff, accordingly, could not be burdened by having to perform all the traditional duties.

For these broader reasons the program operators decided to replace the traditional intake procedure, which usually included separate steps of reception, intake interview, testing, and assignment to vocational counseling, and which resulted in waiting periods, the need for appointments, and frequent delays before actual delivery of services. In its place the new procedure called for assignment of each applicant directly from the reception desk to the next available vocational counselor, who would in turn assign the youth to suitable training or placement services on the same day if possible. The receptionists merely asked the applicant whether he was out of school and if he lived in the area served by the program before directing him to the next counselor available on a rotation basis.

The program operators believed that intensive testing and counseling could be provided to the trainees after they were enrolled in the program and were receiving their training stipends. They further believed that by sharply reducing the delay between reception and assignment to training they would help ensure that more of the easily discouraged youth among the target population would enter the program. Since they were attempting to reach clients who resisted the "waiting game" played at more traditional social agencies, the elimination of the intake process was an important step in that direction.

The program opened its doors with the new intake procedures and began operations without an elaborate central record-keeping procedure that the operators believed might also contribute to delays and divert counselors from their main task of moving youth as quickly as possible into the program's training and placement service. During the first several weeks of operation under these procedures, the number of youth applying to the program far exceeded that anticipated, and thus little systematic evaluation of the new techniques was possible.

IDENTIFICATION OF THE PROBLEM

However, during the second month of the program's operations when their initial shock had worn off, counselors began to describe some problems at their regular staff meetings. In the first place, some reported, a significant number of youngsters sent to them by the receptionist had such severe special problems (mental retardation, physical handicap, etc.) that they could not be assigned to the regular vocational training or job placement services of the program. Since they viewed their primary counseling role as serving those youth who could be accommodated in the program, these counselors suggested that the time required for meeting with these specially handicapped youth was diverting them from their main responsibilities.

Other counselors stated that their training and experience was in specialized fields, such as working with non-English-speaking youth or those with correctional histories. Since they were being assigned clients on a random basis, their specialized skills were only rarely being utilized. Not only would their specialized clientele benefit from being assigned to them, but other groups were, in effect, being denied specialized services by the random intake procedure.

The problem confronting the youth-work program, therefore, was to decide whether the advantages of a speedier, unstructured, and less bureaucratic intake process outweighed the unscreened caseload imposed on the vocational counselors. The counselor's complaints, which suggested that many clients were being denied the potential benefits of a more structured intake process, confronted the program's directors with the question of whether to formalize the intake process and, if so, in what manner and to what extent. But it was clear to all the operators that the original procedure was ineffective in helping to achieve the program's goal of speedy and meaningful service to disadvantaged youth.

COPING WITH THE PROBLEM

The directors of the program considered what minimum background information about a youth was needed to eliminate the inefficiencies reported by the vocational counselors. They determined that perhaps a brief intake interview before assignment to a permanent counselor might produce the gross screening to enable youth with specialized interests or problems to be assigned to the appropriate counselor and also to refer obviously handicapped or ineligible youth to other appropriate agencies.

The program director therefore proposed that each of the vocational counselors be assigned to function as an intake interviewer on a rotating basis. His function would be to interview the clients briefly as they arrived at the reception unit of the agency, eliminate the severely handicapped, and refer those with special problems (such as those with correctional histories or non-English-speaking youth) to the appropriate counselor. All other youth were still to be assigned on a random basis to the first available counselor with time to see a client at that point.

This system of rotating the vocational counselors to serve as ad hoc intake workers was accepted and put into effect after the first two months of operation under the unstructured system. Although this modification was to continue for the next six months, further operational problems soon began to appear. The counselors generally considered their part-time duties in intake as fringe activities somewhat below their professional status, and the effectiveness of their screening was frequently challenged by their supervisors and other counselors. Furthermore the growing requirements of the program operators for files, research, and accurate data revealed that the absence of a formal intake process simply did not permit systematic collection of data on the clients (except for the information the vocational counselors accumulated at subsequent times).

These problems were considered serious enough by the youth-work program directors to request the assistance of an outside consultant. This consultant, after study, recommended the further formalization of the intake process based on the development of a professional intake staff whose sole responsibility would be the initial screening of the clients, maintenance of intake record files, and the assignment of the trainees to the appropriate counselors. These intake counselors, the consultant suggested, should not be given any other counseling duties so that they would be able to devote their full attention to the intake process.

The major reason for this recommendation was that the type of training and skills necessary for effective intake counseling were believed to be different from and more highly specialized than those required for vocational counseling. By hiring specialists with superior skills in these fields, the consultant believed, the inefficiency caused by the "rotation" experience would be reduced.

The major drawback in this recommendation, in the opinion of the program staff, was that budgetary limits would permit the hiring of only two intake counselors. The number would be insufficient to handle the daily intake load, and a system of future appointments (up to a week after reception) would be required if each new applicant was to be interviewed by an intake counselor. The resulting delay in service, of course, was the obstacle the program directors had hoped to overcome through the original unstructured intake process.

Although some of the youth-work program staff objected to the recommendation on the grounds that it was imposing a bureaucratic structure on the agency's flexible procedures, it was accepted by the director because of its potential value to data collection and more effective matching of youth to training programs. The specialized intake counselors were employed nine months after the program first began operations.

Shortly thereafter, the impact of the more formalized intake procedure became evident. Since the youth were all given a specific appointment time by the receptionists to meet with one of the two intake counselors, there were delays of up to several weeks and some of them did not return. Thus a significant rise in the number of dropouts between reception and assignment to an intake counselor was reported. Unkept appointments resulted in unutilized time for the counselors and, as the problems of the appointment system multiplied, some applicants had to wait several weeks for intake interviews. The program directors then permitted intake counselors with broken appointments to see any youngster waiting in the reception unit, and this "backup" appointment system reduced the waiting period (and therefore the dropout rate) to some degree.

CONSEQUENCES

It required about one year of operation for the youth-work program to move from a system stressing quick assignment of all youngsters who entered the reception unit of the agency to a relatively structured, formalized intake procedure bridging the gap between reception and vocational counseling. The program operators had discovered that their experiment with an unstructured intake process did not benefit the clients as much as they had anticipated, while at the same time it produced serious additional problems for agency operation. In an effort to overcome these additional problems, the operators decided, step by step, to establish a structured intake process with its attendant system of appointments and delays and which confronted the youngster with an imposing array of counselors, interviews, and forms to be completed.

QUESTIONS FOR DISCUSSION

1. Do you agree with the assumptions on which the program operators based their initial decision to eliminate the intake process?

2. Were these program operators naive in their belief that they could avoid bureaucratization?

3. What do you consider to be the advantages and disadvantages of a highly structured intake process?

4. Did the emergence of the final specialized intake procedure follow inevitably from the prior decision to establish the rotation of intake counseling?

Consolidation versus Specialization of Counseling Functions: A Dilemma for a Youth-Work Program

During the planning period, a comprehensive youth-work program decided to provide its services to each youth through the assignment of one counselor who was to be responsible for helping him to use all aspects of the program. Within a relatively short time after operations began, however, it was found that despite random assignment of clients to counselors widely varying patterns of services were being provided. Since the only evident variable was the counselors themselves, it was determined that differences in patterns of counselor functioning caused these problems.

Efforts to cope with the problems included intensive staff training, a reorganization of the intake process to differentiate trainees needing prevocational training from those ready for job placement, a differentiation of counselor responsibilities between placement and training functions, a six-month time limit on training, and finally, the assignment of specialized placement counselors to trainees in the final month of training.

The result of these efforts was a significant change in the numbers of trainees being moved on to more advanced job or training situations, but the original planning goal of maintaining an ongoing individual counselor-client relationships had been discarded.

BACKGROUND

Planners of a youth-work demonstration project designed to serve a racially mixed slum area in a large city, consciously tried to avoid the overspecialization of staff functions so typical in health and welfare services. This comprehensive program included, in addition to supportive services, prevocational, on-the-job and job placement services, and work training conducted through work crews. It began operation in October, 1963.

The work crews were composed of 12 to 18 trainees supervised in their vocational training (e.g., auto repair, food preparation, building repair, and woodworking) by crew foremen, who typically were experienced workers in the various trades. The central coordinating role in the program was to be played by 20 professional counselors, who were to be assigned approximately 50 trainees at random during the intake process and assume continuous responsibility for helping these youth plan and carry out their vocational programs. They were to determine first whether a youth was ready for immediate job placement, whether remedial education or health services were required, and to which work crew he should be assigned for work training. In short each youth was to relate to only one professional, who would not only guide his progress through the program, but would also provide ongoing counseling.

The program planners were aware that such a consolidation of counseling functions might not take full advantage of the specialized previous training and competence of some counselors. They foresaw especially that the higher status of counselors coming from rehabilitation or psychiatric backgrounds (relative to those with vocational and job placement backgrounds) might lead to problems within the framework of the desired consolidation of functions, but they were willing to take the risk. During the planning process, the presumed advantages of the one-to-one counselor/client relationship in assuring continuity of service outweighed any of its possible disadvantages.

When the program opened its doors, youngsters from the slum area —a majority of them Puerto Ricans between sixteen and twenty-two —began entering the program at an annual rate of 2,000. The 20 counselors, who were drawn from a variety of educational and work backgrounds but were all experienced professionals, were assigned clients on a random basis and given responsibility for delivery of *all* services for their caseloads.

IDENTIFICATION OF THE PROBLEM

Within six months after the program began operation, the administrators of the youth-work program became aware that too many trainees were still in work crews and not enough were being placed in regular jobs. The rates of client turnover among the counselors varied widely. Some counselors seemed always able to accept new clients, but others seemed to maintain a relatively stable caseload. The administrators speculated that the counselors with high turnover rates tended to place youngsters directly in jobs and to bypass prevocational training entirely, while counselors with low turnover rates tended to retain their clients in the work crews and hesitated to move them on to regular employment.

In an effort to test these impressions, the program administrators conducted a survey of the counselors and their caseloads, which in general confirmed their earlier impressions. In addition the survey revealed that counselors with backgrounds in the rehabilitation field were more reluctant to recommend that their clients were ready for job placement than counselors with employment service and other placement-oriented backgrounds, who tended to move their clients quickly to outside jobs.

The survey also indicated that the placement-oriented counselors tended to view job placement as the crucial goal of the program. If disadvantaged youth had jobs, they believed, their other needs would tend to diminish or would be met more easily by the youths themselves. The training-oriented counselors, on the other hand, felt most strongly that their clients needed a relatively extensive amount of preparation before they were ready for regular employment. At the extremes the placement group saw employment as an end in itself, while the training group visualized intensive training for long-range vocational goals as the major purpose of the program.

COPING WITH THE PROBLEM

For the administrators of the youth-work program, a major problem was the small number of youngsters being placed in regular employment. Since permanent placement was the expressed goal of their program, their attention was focused first on those trainees who seemed to be "stuck" in the work crews. It was determined that these trainees did not differ significantly in age, education, and previous work experience from those who were being placed in jobs. Further, differences in job placement rates did not appear to be related to the nature of the work performed by work crews. There was no formal time limit for participation in this program, so trainees remained in the crews until the counselor decided they were ready to move into regular employment.

The only remaining variable, the counselors themselves, was therefore identified as the major cause of the problem, since the study had absolved both the trainees and the crew foremen. The administrators further concluded that the problem was caused by the different backgrounds and previous professional training of the counselors, as well as by their varying perspectives toward jobs and work training. The placement-oriented counselors, again, saw regular employment as the best way for youngsters to cope with their various problems, while the training-oriented counselors believed their clients primarily needed training, remedial education, and individual counseling, and that a job per se would not provide long-range answers to their problems.

The survey also indicated that there was apparently little difference between the rates of successful job placements (defined impressionistically as the small number of youngsters returning to the agency for further job help) made by training- and placement-oriented counselors. In short, youngsters placed directly on the job at intake and those placed after prevocational training did not appear to fare significantly differently.

A further conclusion drawn by the program administrators was that some of the training-oriented counselors tended to fear making "premature" job placements (that is, unsuccessful placements) and therefore continued youths in sheltered work-crew training in order to avoid expected failures. It was also found that some trainees feared failure in regular employment. The relatively comfortable environment of the work crews made regular employment appear even less attractive. Thus the orientation of the counselors and the attitude of the trainees toward work seemed to be related.

The administrators concluded that the approach of the training-oriented counselors, which emphasized intensive preparation and minimized immediate employment, was an important factor inhibiting them from recommending job placement for their trainees. On the other hand, the placement-oriented counselors had no such inhibition. Indeed, they were in a sense protected by their view that employment was a positive and necessary experience even if the youngster returned to the agency after a short time. These counselors tended to try again without developing anxiety or inhibitions about making placement.

The program administrators' first attempt to cope with the problem of varying counselor orientation was to provide more intensive staff supervision and training. They hoped, through this process, to develop a more consistent approach by all counselors and to minimize extreme attitudes in both groups. Some of the administrative staff, however, argued that the problem lay far deeper. They proposed that some reorganization of the consolidated counseling structure was required, even if some separation of functions would result.

Within another three months, it became clear that closer supervision and training alone would not solve the problem, as caseloads continued to vary according to the orientation of the counselors. If supervision and training were to succeed, it became clear, a long-range effort would be needed to reorient the counselors, and the time required was simply not available in this demonstration project.

In the fall of 1964, one year after the program began operation, the youth-work administrators reached general agreement that the intake process needed to be reorganized and specialized. Taking the original responsibility for determining work readiness away from all counselors, the administrators established a separate intake unit to judge which youths were ready for immediate job placement and which needed prior experience in the work crews. This step was the first formal departure from the consolidated role for the counselors; it established the first separation of functions. The counselors now took responsibility for the trainees only after intake processing, and the continuity of service from intake to job placement with which the program began operations was thus broken.

The second aspect of the reorganization took the work-training component out of the hands of the placement-oriented counselors. Their sole responsibility now was to counsel those youngsters judged ready for placement by the intake workers and to attempt to place them on jobs. Training-oriented counselors were now assigned to those youngsters judged by the intake workers as needing work-crew experience. These counselors were also responsible for deciding at what point the trainees were ready for job placement and for making the placement itself. The placement counselors reacted sharply against this decision, since in effect it reduced their status. Their responsibilities had now been reduced to job-hunting and placement while the training counselors maintained control over both training and placement.

The first reorganization had several positive results, however, according to the program administrators. They believed it provided a better chance for proper initial referral, since by determining readiness for work through systematic testing and an evaluative intake process, it avoided the differing perspectives and consequent subjective decisions of the two main groups of counselors. At the same time, it permitted better use of the specialized training and backgrounds of the counselors.

However, one of the specific problems remained. The training-oriented counselors continued to hold trainees in the work crews for what appeared to be unduly long periods of time. In some cases they did not accept the crew foremen's recommendations for job placement of trainees who had already learned enough of the vocational skills required for regular employment. The administrators concluded that more measures were necessary to overcome the training counselors' apparent continuing fears of failure.

The administrators then decided to impose a six-month limit on the time a trainee could spend in a work crew in an effort to increase the number of job placements. If a counselor insisted on retaining a youngster beyond this time, he could request an extension, but the burden would now be on the counselor to justify such a recommendation against job placement. The decision produced very strong opposition from the training counselors, who felt it implicitly questioned their judgment.

But imposition of the six-month time limit also failed to resolve the problem. The maximum became the minimum in effect, as counselors tended to retain the trainees in the work crews for six months before beginning seriously to consider their level of readiness for regular employment. Extensions were frequently requested.

At this point, the program administrators decided that an additional cause of the problem was the lack of information about labor market conditions on the part of the training counselors. Unlike the placement counselors, they had less knowledge about the types of jobs, the working conditions, and other situations that their clients might encounter after leaving the program. Coupled with their persistent fear of the trainee's failure and the fact that their rate of successful placements was not high, the problems of the training counselors could not be resolved, in the opinion of the program administrators, without further change in the organization of counseling functions.

Accordingly the administrators decided to give part of the responsibility for placement counseling during the final (sixth) month of a trainee's work-crew experience to a placement-oriented counselor. This meant a further differentiation of counseling functions, since the training counselors now would control only the training component, whereas placement counselors would work jointly with the training counselors during the final month and take continuing responsibility when a trainee's work-crew experience terminated.

This second reorganization of counseling functions was, in effect, an effort to move trainees more rapidly out of the sheltered work crews and into the real world of work. By elimination of youngsters who did not appear to need work experience at intake, the work crews were primarily receiving those who would benefit from work training. By imposing a six-month time limit on the trainees' stay and bringing a placement counselor into joint responsibility for their final month, and finally, into full responsibility for placement itself, the program administrators hoped to move trainees into regular employment more effectively and to utilize fully the varying orientations of the counseling staff.

Some of the trainees themselves, however, reacted to such measures with a phenomenon described as "employment shock." Work-crew foremen and training counselors first recognized it in youth who were faced with separation from the work crew and who were expected to make the transition to the working world outside. Periodic trainee progress reports by crew foremen in the final week of training and informal statements made at general staff and supervisory meetings revealed a deterioration of interest, work performance, behavior, and attendance in many of these youths. Both training counselors and placement counselors noticed other symptoms which were discussed with the counseling supervisor on an individual basis. There were reports of anxiety and fearfulness in trainees at the prospect of not finding employment. Many failed to keep their appointments with the placement counselor. Some trainees themselves requested extensions beyond the six-month time limit. At the initiative of the counseling supervisor, a series of group-counseling sessions, conducted by both the training and placement counselors, were held in an effort to relieve "employment shock," and some progress was noted by the program administrators.

CONSEQUENCES

In the judgment of the program administrators, the series of four separate decisions to cope with the consequences of a consolidated counseling system ultimately showed a significant improvement in the number of youngsters placed in more appropriate situations and an increase in the likelihood of more successful transitions from the sheltered work crews to regular jobs. The administrators concluded that, in the words of one of them, "if we had to do this all over again, we would have begun with a separation of counseling functions." In their view the disadvantages of consolidated functions far outweighed its advantages, such as continuity of personal contact between the trainee and the counselor.

QUESTIONS FOR DISCUSSION

1. Is the consolidation of counseling functions a desirable goal?

2. If an administrator wanted to achieve consolidation, what could he have done differently in planning or operating this program?

3. Do you agree with the administrator's diagnosis of "the problem"?

4. What is your assessment of the positive or negative consequences of the solution described?

5. Do you identify yourself with the approach attributed to the "placement-oriented" counselors or with that attributed to the "training-oriented" counselors?

A Problem of Diagnosis: A Bonding Program Fails to Produce New Job Opportunities

卐卐

After extensive study, federal planners designed an experimental program to subsidize commercial bonding for youth and adults whose police records appeared to prevent their bonding, leading to employment in a wide variety of jobs. The program was based upon the assumption that enabling applicants with police records to be bonded would overcome the obstacle to regular employment for a significant number of disadvantaged youth and adults. Several community youth-work agencies were invited by a federal agency to participate in this experimental program. Their experience of offering to provide such bonding to employers, however, resulted in a disappointingly small number of acceptances by employers.

After almost a year of efforts to test the effectiveness of the bonding program, at least one local program operator concluded that the bonding requirement mentioned by many employers during original job development contacts was in fact merely another screening method, designed to ensure the selection of the most "desirable." Another local program operator concluded from this experience that the real obstacle to employment of youth with police records was the employer's access to the records themselves and the fact he could require the information from the applicant as a condition of employment.

BACKGROUND

Among the barriers to the employment of disadvantaged youth has been the frequent requirement by employers that applicants even for relatively unskilled jobs, such as clerking in a department store or delivering, be bonded. Fidelity bonding insures the employer from financial loss as a result of employee theft. Employment service counselors and operators of youth-work programs have frequently reported that commercial bonding companies usually refuse to issue bonds for youth with police records, often without regard to the nature of the offense or its disposition.

For example one of the few research studies of this problem, conducted in Washington, D.C., by an independent researcher, found that of more than 5,000 job applicants to a local manpower program 85 per cent of the males and 10 per cent of the females had police records. A concurrent analysis of more than 5,000 job openings generated by the same program's job developers revealed that 42.5 per cent required some form of "police clearance," which implied that employers would rarely hire an applicant with a record and would require a commercial bond.

The Washington study recommended "the establishment of a bonding system that will grant bonds to people with police records so that this obstacle toward securing employment would be overcome." As a result, an experimental program of federally subsidized bonding was established by the Office of Manpower Policy, Evaluation and Research of the U.S. Department of Labor in 1966. Arguing for the program before a congressional committee, Labor Secretary W. Willard Wirtz stated, "After we train them, they have trouble getting a job because an employer looks at that (police) record and feels it is a risk he cannot take." Fidelity bonding, he continued, would effectively reduce this risk and open a large number of previously closed jobs to the disadvantaged youth and adults of the nation.

In June of 1966, community manpower programs in four large cities were invited by OMPER to administer an experimental bonding program. Their role was to approach employers who had previously indicated that bonding was a condition of employment for their current entry-level job openings. They were then to propose that a specific applicant, whose individual background the job developers presented to the employer, be hired. The employer was to be informed that the applicant, although not bondable by a commercial firm, could now be bonded under the new federal program. If the employer consented to hire the applicant, the job developer was to prepare an application to a commercial bonding company, which would bill the Department of Labor at an agreed-upon rate.

IDENTIFICATION OF THE PROBLEM

One of the four agencies selected by OMPER to administer the bonding program in a large metropolitan area was an organization committed to serving delinquent and delinquency-prone youth. In the first month after starting to participate in the program, the agency's job developers had contacted 40 employers who previously had indicated that bonding was a condition of employment. Somewhat surprisingly, these employers consistently responded to the job developer's recommendation that a particular unskilled youth be hired by saying they now needed semiskilled or skilled workers—not the unskilled applicants for whom entry-level jobs were being sought. An additional reason for not accepting the now bondable applicants was that all the employees had to be bonded by a company designated by the employer, which was not the one which OMPER had contracted with. A small number of these same employers did, however, provide agency applicants with jobs but, interestingly, without requiring bonding. One major maintenance company stated it required applicants to be more than twenty-five years old (older than the group served by the agency) and that none could have police records, regardless of their bondability under the new program.

Thus the experience of the agency, which continued to participate in the program for the following year, indicated that only a handful of employers were interested. The problem confronting the agency, then, was to determine why the program was not being utilized and draw conclusions for future action.

COPING WITH THE PROBLEM

The first conclusion drawn by the agency was that the bonding requirement was not in itself an actual condition of employment for most employers approached. Instead its staff agreed that it served as a convenient screening device to reduce a perceived risk for employers in hiring workers with police records. The fact that an applicant was not commercially bondable served as evidence that he had a police record or other undesirable characteristics, and employers wished to avoid hiring such youth as long as they had other applicants. In short, bonding requirements reflected employer attitudes of preference for the most highly qualified worker at any given level of position. In this context, bonding was used as a convenient way to eliminate the least desirable applicants for employment, in the same manner as educational requirements, test results, and other screening devices.

The job developers of another agency participating in the demonstration, while reporting similarly poor results with youth, did report better results for older semiskilled and skilled workers who had police records. Since such skilled workers were in short supply, employers were willing to accept bonding through the federal program and thus actually did provide some new job opportunities. But for disadvantaged youth with little skill or experience, bonding in itself did not appear to be the critical barrier to employment.

CONSEQUENCES

Throughout the country, in the four participating cities, only 54 applicants had been bonded under the program in the first nine months of operation, and 15 of these had terminated their employment shortly after their first placement. For a program initially funded at $500,000 for two years, the results were disappointing.

Based on their conclusions that bonding requirements were frequently only a screening device used by employers, rather than an actual condition of employment, the youth-work program operators decided that other techniques would have to be used to cope with the real issue presented by the apparent failure of the experimental bonding program. This real issue was the ability of employers to secure access to police or court records and their ability to use arrest records as a basic condition of employment, even if such arrests did not result in convictions. If this barrier to the employment of disadvantaged youth was to be overcome, a different technique would have to be developed.

A suggestion offered by legal staff members and job developers in the youth-work agency was, first, to seek legal and administrative action to ensure confidentiality of police and court records, especially for juveniles, and, second, to prevent employers, through legislative or administrative reforms, from inquiring of prospective employees whether they had ever been arrested. Since arrest is rarely followed by conviction for a large number of juveniles, the staff members concluded that such techniques might offer more promise of new employment opportunities than the bonding program.

QUESTIONS FOR DISCUSSION

1. What other steps could have been taken to diagnose the "real" problem without undertaking the experimental bonding program?

2. As a diagnostic tool for planning purposes, should the demonstration be considered a success?

3. What could the job developers have done when they realized that employers were using bonding as a screen?

4. Were employers behaving irresponsibly in their desire to screen out applicants who had police records?

5. Should employers be denied the right to ask about an applicant's police record?

PROBLEMS OF ORGANIZATIONAL CHANGE

ꙮꙮ   *Introduction to the Cases*

After 1960 a marked change became apparent in the thinking of those
who were shaping federal programs in the fields of juvenile delinquency, youth unemployment, and the broader problems of poverty.
Simply stated, these planners recognized that if any of these social
problems were to be solved, significant changes would be required in
the existing organization of services for the severely disadvantaged
portions of the population. In the past, they believed, these groups
consistently had not received their fair share of health, legal, educational, recreational, welfare, and vocational services, to mention but a
few.

These planners concluded that merely providing additional funds
to expand the existing organization and delivery of these services
would achieve little of lasting significance. Although of course there
was full awareness that organizations inevitably change, the social and
political climate at the time reflected an increasing popular impa-
tience and a desire to increase the rate of change through planned

intervention into organizational structures. This sense of urgency was underlined by the growing militance of the civil rights movement and found expression in some of the new legislation, particularly in the mandate of the Economic Opportunity Act for "maximum feasible participation" of the poor.

In response to these pressures a new goal of organizational change began to emerge. Its proponents among federal planners believed that providing more effective services might require that some existing organizations close, that others develop new goals, that still others create new methods of delivering services, and lastly that new organizations be created where modification of existing ones would not be possible. A number of the recent federal programs planned from this new perspective had specifically identified organizational change as their primary goal, and the change they sought was not only to provide some specific new service but perhaps more importantly to affect the basic organization and delivery of needed services over the long run. For example, Project Headstart was viewed by its sponsors in the Office of Economic Opportunity as one way to affect the general manner in which education is provided across the country to the poor and minority groups. The Youth Opportunity Centers, sponsored by the Department of Labor, represented an effort to produce change in the various state employment services. And the pressure for organizational change was not limited to the federal agencies alone; new community programs also adopted these new goals and worked to achieve them on the local level.

Unfortunately the commitment to the goal of organizational change has not been accompanied by the emergence of a systematic body of knowledge concerning the strategies through which such change was to be produced. Consequently, in the past few years, many serious efforts have been launched, considerable community conflict created, and much worthwhile organizational change achieved, although through different strategies and tactics.

Increasing attention, however, is now being paid to these techniques of achieving organizational change, which include direct confrontation and conflict, the use of money as leverage, appeals to mutual self-interest, negotiation, exhortation, and demonstration of new and more effective service methods. The one common obstacle that all these techniques have had to overcome is the apparent tendency of all organizations to resist change. And while knowledge and experience in these areas is far from complete, it seems clear that the technique used will generally reflect the power relationships which exist between the change "agent" and the change "target." Where the change agent enjoys full control of the target, it may achieve organizational change through the issuance of direct orders; where power clearly rests with the target of change, the technique employed by the agent is more likely to involve the patient demonstration of benefits for the target.

Since the existing power relationship between change agents and targets usually falls within these extremes (and more often than not favors the target), the most common techniques for achieving organizational change when the agents possess some degree of leverage has been through the use of funds. These funds have been used both to establish new programs and to reorganize or expand existing ones. When the relationship approaches an equilibrium, the agent must promise some benefits or resources, such as an expanded clientele or enhanced prestige, as well as rely on persuasion and exhortation. Finally, when the power relationship favors the target, such benefits must be clearly demonstrated, not simply promised, and the final decision to change is reserved for the target.

Techniques of resistance selected by the change targets similarly reflect the power relationship. If the target possesses a clearly favorable balance of power, it can reject proposed programs outright, or insist on fully controlling them and later adapt only those aspects that have clearly proved beneficial. With the power relationship at equilibrium, the target may attempt to negotiate some degree of control, or it can utilize its position to reduce the amount of change it will accept. Finally, the weak target may be forced to accept the patina of change and rely on its organizational strength to reduce the impact.

The cases presented in this chapter illustrate all these techniques of organizational change as well as resistance, against a background of the continuum of power relationships. Some of the efforts described were carefully planned; others made use of unexpected opportunities.

But all were launched by planners of social services committed to the new concepts of organizational change.

In the first case we see an example of a carefully planned, shared effort between segments of a local community and a department of the federal government to broadly affect the patterns of the delivery of services by a group of well-established public and private organizations in a community. The technique used by the federal and local change agents to achieve change was the use of federal funds to create agency commitment to organizational change (a commitment which was central to the new organization but not likely to have been shared by the existing agencies). Although the new agency did not have the power to direct the local agencies to change, it did possess a certain amount of prestige as a result of having been chosen by the federal agency to receive an initial planning grant. But more importantly it was in the position to influence the direction of flow of federal funds to the existing agencies. And here it had significant ability to affect change, which it chose to use by shunning direct conflict and substituting the leverage of money.

This case illustrates a decision by the agent of change to use existing structures rather than to create new or parallel ones. It is also an example of a technique which combines appeals to mutual self-interest with the power to influence the flow of funds. In addition the case illustrates the resistance technique through which well-established agencies use their power to negotiate for the new funds while retaining control of their use. One wonders, however, what would have been the outcome in this case if the new central agency had pressed for changes which the existing agencies felt to be unacceptable. In such an event, one might speculate that the established agencies would have coped with this threat, not through accommodation, but rather through the more open exercise of their power.

The second case is an example of one specific public organization, a state employment service, as the target of change by a newly created private agency. The private agency possessed neither a preponderance of power nor new funds and so, not surprisingly, the change technique it selected was one requiring negotiation, demonstration, and, most important, an appeal to self-interest. It relied heavily upon the participation of the ES staff in a newly created experimental program, hoping to influence these staff members by such direct exposure and, through them, their larger organization. The private agency believed that the ES agreed to participate in the program because it wished to modify its public image and saw such joint involvement as one way to move into more flexible and professional methods of delivering its services. But the ES's insistence on retaining supervisory control of its out-stationed staff illustrated its relatively strong position in the power relationship.

In assessing the techniques of achieving and resisting change employed in this case, which relied almost exclusively on the participation of the staff of the target agency in a change agent's program, one is struck by the clarity with which the goals of organizational change are identified, but at the same time the absence of any clearly delineated methods of achieving them.

In the third case, however, we see a more systematic attempt to bring about change from a position of far greater power through the involvement of staff. Here a federal agency undertook a deliberate and centrally planned effort to produce change in its state affiliates. It wished to ensure that more disadvantaged youth receive its services, but equally it wanted to change these organizations in such a way that would produce more effective services for adults as well. The federal agency possessed little real power to order state agencies to change, but it could control the flow of new money. So it too avoided confrontation and selected a strategy in which it hoped to achieve change by: (1) providing money for the expansion of state services and thereby creating a need for additional staff, (2) providing money for training this staff, (3) controlling the selection of "non-Establishment" students to participate in training, (4) controlling the actual content of their training, and (5) establishing guidelines for the delivery of service under the expanded program.

We see in this case quite a clear description of the methodology employed by a federal agency as well as an excellent account of how the target of change, possessing less power but retaining administrative control of the new programs, was able to assimilate new staff and programs without fundamentally altering its structure and goals.

Organizational change, as the consequence of a specific demonstration effort, is described in the fourth case. Here we see a process unfold in which a researcher, in order to demonstrate a new instructional method, sought an operating program to serve as his laboratory. In order to safeguard his demonstration, he realized that certain organizational changes needed to be made which he was now in the position to influence as a result of his successful demonstration. At this point the research director seized upon the unexpected opportunity and decided to shift his earlier focus from research to that of broader organizational change. Here the lack of power or money by the change agent dictated a strategy which avoided conflict and maximized an appeal to the organization's self-interest—a more effective teaching program at less cost in teaching and custodial personnel. This is an example of the ease with which organizational change can take place where the organization sees nothing but benefit accruing to it as a result of the change. Unfortunately this happy circumstance is the exception rather than the rule. The outcome of this might well have been different if, in order to accommodate the new teaching method, the correctional institution would have had to commit more of its resources rather than less.

In the final case of youth training in a hospital we see a modest demonstration conducted by an outside agency in one hospital through which it hopes to have a larger impact upon the utilization of nonprofessional personnel in the broader hospital field. The outside agency, with little power to directly affect this huge field, chose as its method the conduct of a successful demonstration of benefits to the hospital. In contrast to the previous case, this demonstration was seen as instrumental to the achievement of the broader goal, but in both cases organizational change was required to ensure the success of the demonstration. When roadblocks emerged, the director of the demonstration program had to decide whether or not to permit them to become conflict issues and attempt to resolve them as such. Clearly the decision was made to avoid open conflict and to accept difficult conditions in the hope that a successful demonstration along with the involvement of hospital personnel would reduce the organization's resistance to further needed change.

The decision-maker in this case was faced with deciding whether or not the conditions established by the hospital, with its greater power, were so restrictive as to limit the possibility of carrying out even a moderately successful program. If the training program had failed, such failure might have produced a self-fulfilling prophecy on the part of the hospital which in turn might well have foreclosed any further effort at organizational change.

Who Will Operate the Programs? The Decisions of a Planning Organization Promoting Organizational Change

卐卐

A social planning and action corporation, established before the enactment of Community Action Program legislation in the Economic Opportunity Act, was planning a comprehensive youth-work program to be financed on a demonstration basis by federal funds. One of the goals of the local corporation, and of the federal agencies, was to explore how federal funds, channeled through a local planning agency, could help redirect the programs of established social agencies toward the problems of disadvantaged youth. In this planning process the local corporation was faced with making a series of decisions concerning which, if any, established community agencies in the field it would invite to operate the various components of the program.

In the course of this planning process, three major influences on the corporation's decisions are identified: (1) the expressed goals of the corporation itself, (2) the interests and requirements of the federal funding agencies, and (3) the interests and influence of the various community agencies competing for participation in the program (and, therefore, for ensuing funds). Finally, after confronting varying combinations of these major influences, the corporation selected a total of eight established agencies, four public and four private, to operate the various components of the program and decided to operate three components itself.

BACKGROUND

During 1961 and 1962, a group of political, civic, and welfare agency leaders in a large city, initially brought together in response to the difficulties and opportunities presented by a large-scale urban renewal program, were attempting to establish a community development corporation for community-wide social planning and action. The corporation was being organized during a period of growing Negro demands for a wide range of social services, of general concern about the social and economic problems of the community, and of both implicit and explicit criticism of the way established employment, education, welfare, health, and other service programs were being operated.

The founders of the corporation were members of the "establishment," yet were dissidents within it. They wanted to bring about changes in the policies and practices of both the public and private agencies in the community, primarily by encouraging them to shift their resources and attention to the problems of the inner city and its predominantly low-income Negro population. These were also the goals of a national philanthropic foundation and the President's Committee on Juvenile Delinquency, which were developing the climate and strategy for a number of experimental efforts to achieve organizational change in established social welfare agencies at the community level. When the prospect of substantial amounts of federal and foundation funds for such purposes became known, the corporation's founders attempted to plan the precise combination of goals, programs, and organizational structure that would meet the criteria of the potential funding sources.

The corporation drew up a grant proposal specifically for planning and developing a program to control juvenile delinquency. But it was not the only organization in the city interested in receiving federal and private funds for this purpose, and a sharp competition developed among several local agencies, one of which was the municipal bureau charged with the responsibility of working with delinquents. The corporation won the struggle, however, and received a planning and development grant from the Office of Juvenile Delinquency (OJD) of the Department of Health, Education, and Welfare in December of 1963. Although the corporation emerged victorious from the competition, it had to agree to the condition proposed by a federal agency that it establish a program advisory committee consisting primarily of representatives of the agencies that had been disappointed.

Funds available from the OJD for program implementation, however, were severely limited, as was its influence on the larger and more established federal bureaucracies whose programs and resources were addressed to such urban social problems as youth employment. It was therefore a happy discovery when the corporation found that the Office of Manpower, Automation, and Training (OMAT, now OMPER) of the Department of Labor would agree to making funds available for youth-work programs, and to channeling them through such new anti-delinquency agencies as the corporation. Further, it was learned that OMAT had some definite notions, similar in concept to those of the OJD, about the kind of community youth-work demonstration programs that should be developed and the impact it wished them to have on established agencies.

A meeting was arranged in the city between representatives of OMAT, the corporation, and the state employment service, and a series of conferences were held with other local employment-related agencies. A demonstration program was agreed upon, and a contract was signed for its operation between OMAT and the corporation. The program was to be a comprehensive youth-work program, directed toward disadvantaged youth in the city, with the following components (in addition to administration): (1) recruitment (2) intake and individual assessment (3) counseling (4) work orientation (5) remedial education (6) intensive evaluation and conditioning (7) skill training (8) job placement (9) job development (10) research.

IDENTIFICATION OF THE PROBLEM

During the planning period, the corporation was faced with a series of basic questions regarding the development of its youth-work program. They included: Which local agencies will be used to operate the program? Will they be established agencies or new ones created specifically for this program? Will coordination be implemented on a cooperative voluntary basis or through formal written contracts? Underlying all these was the basic strategy for organizational change adopted by both the corporation and the interested federal agencies: the channeling of funds to established agencies in exchange for a new emphasis on disadvantaged, mainly Negro youth and new comprehensive services for this target population.

The corporation's decisions on these crucial problems were made under the influence of three major forces: (1) the interests and requirements of the funding agencies of the federal government, (2) the corporation's own goals, and (3) the power and interests of the various local agencies. These will be examined separately below.

COPING WITH THE PROBLEM

The federal government, acting through OMAT and the OJD, had set the broad goals and was the source of funds for the youth-work program. It was therefore the most important of the three major influences, and the corporation had to be sensitive to the signals from Washington regarding the shape and content of the local program. As the main lines of the program emerged through successive drafts, federal expectations became increasingly explicit and were translated into program components.

The emphasis given to one component or another and the techniques to be used were subject to changes during the planning period as federal officials hammered out policies under the pressure of launching new programs across the country. Guidelines and expectations shifted as the federal administrators encountered unanticipated difficulties and found unexpected resources.

In order to give the program the emphasis they considered important, the OMAT representatives specifically recommended to the corporation the use of certain agencies to carry out parts of the program. These recommendations were accepted with alacrity by the corporation because they came from the source of funding and were perceived and interpreted as requirements, not mere suggestions. The corporation's ready acceptance of the word from Washington, however, led to strains locally when an excluded agency asked the corporation for an explanation of its exclusion. In short, the tasks to be performed under the new youth-work program were determined in large part by federal guidelines. In at least two instances, noted below, the corporation included or excluded specific agencies from participation in response to federal "suggestions."

Well before the stimulation of the youth-work program by OMAT and the OJD, the corporation had adopted an explicit policy that all new programs would be implemented by existing agencies whenever one could be found that was willing and equipped, in the opinion of the corporation, to assume the responsibility. This was consistent with the corporation's view of itself as a stimulator of organizational change rather than a competitor with the established social service agencies. The corporation expected to devote its energies not to providing direct services but to helping established organizations take on new experimental programs by providing them with planning, research, and financial assistance as a coordinating "umbrella" agency. Only when there was no other course was it anticipated that the corporation would deviate from this policy of "maximum feasible participation" of existing agencies and operate program components itself.

Within the constraints of federal pressures and the corporation's own policies, local factors and inter-organizational relationships had influence on which agencies were given what responsibilities. Some public agencies had legal responsibilities for certain program components; some private agencies were extremely vocal in their demands to be included in the program; and others had certain positive advantages in geographic location, experience, and specific areas of specialization. All three influences were usually combined to affect the corporation's eventual decisions on which specific agencies would operate the various program components.

The three major influences on the decisions made by the corporation as the designated "umbrella" agency resulted in the following allocations of the youth-work program's components:

Recruitment. The city's delinquency control agency was given responsibility for recruitment of disadvantaged youth and for certain follow-up functions. The decision was made by the corporation primarily to pay the political debt incurred when, as an active challenger to the corporation for the OJD planning grant, it stood aside. In return the corporation agreed to provide it with new funds and enlarged functions, so the decision to grant it funds and responsibility for recruitment was an implementation of this agreement. Straightforward and direct as this exchange was, it was never made public. The city agency's enlarged responsibilities improved its competitive status vis-à-vis other city agencies.

Intake and assessment, counseling, and work orientation. Federal pressure excluded one agency from consideration for the counseling and testing component because, OMAT believed, it had not shown competence in the field previously, and the corporation accepted this evaluation.

The two settlement houses chosen for these functions were located in low-income neighborhoods and had some limited experience in this area. Both aggressively sought inclusion in the program. The corporation's decision to include them was a result in part of the positive factors of their location and experience and of the settlement's aggressiveness. Since the corporation's own goals included a strong desire to include private agencies in its program for organizational change, the decision to include the settlements appeared to result from both the corporation's goals and their own influence, after the field had been narrowed, in effect, by a federal veto.

Remedial education. The corporation and the federal agencies agreed that the public schools were legally responsible for remedial education in the program, although the schools protested that it would be difficult for them to deliver this service without receiving additional funds.

Intensive evaluation and conditioning. This component was included in the program at federal insistence. OMAT representatives urged that intensive services be available for the most "difficult" clients and strongly recommended one agency to be utilized for this purpose. The agency, OMAT said, had an excellent background and experience in highly individualized counseling and conditioning.

Federal influence was the major factor in the selection of this private vocational counseling agency for the program.

One other private agency was insistent in offering its services. Since intensive counseling was the most specialized (and costly) service included in the youth-work program, the corporation had few alternatives from which to choose. The final decision to utilize two of the private vocational agencies (the one suggested by OMAT and the "insistent" one) was influenced by the corporation's desire to avoid the community repercussions expected to occur if the contract was given to only one agency, and also by its interest in determining which agency could do the most effective job.

Skill training. The state vocational education office insisted that it had legal responsibility for approving all training arrangements. Its approval of the program was also required in view of its relationship with the Labor Department, which insisted that the corporation obtain "voc ed's" concurrence with the youth-work program.

Job placement. The decision here was made on grounds identical to those in the skill training component, except that the public agency insisted upon by OMAT was the state employment service.

Job development and research. For both of these components, as well as overall administrative responsibility for the youth-work program, the corporation was unable to find any established agencies which it considered qualified to undertake these functions. And since there were no special federal or local agency pressures for operating these components the corporation assumed them itself.

In addition to formal contracts, the corporation also made inter-agency arrangements to open channels for referral with the public welfare department and other agencies and with federal and other training resources, as well as for referrals to the state rehabilitation commission. It was considered mutually advantageous to make these arrangements on a voluntary and cooperative basis without the necessity for contracts or financial support. Responsibilities for the new program were also allocated by the corporation and the participating agencies on the basis of an exchange of benefits, a quid pro quo, among organizations.

CONSEQUENCES

Both the federal agencies and the corporation wanted to pull some of the established local agencies into new patterns and methods of delivering new services. In short, their goal was organizational change. In exchange the corporation offered them the incentive of funds and the prestige attached to participating in one of the early anti-poverty efforts. For their part, the participating agencies saw this as an opportunity to expand their functions, obtain new resources, and improve their public relations. In return they offered what the corporation lacked, the facilities and experience to operate the program.

Assumption of the intake, assessment, and other tasks in the program helped the settlement houses to meet criticisms that were then being made locally and nationally about settlements. Their critics had charged that the settlement movement had been reduced to running children's recreation centers and was unresponsive to many basic problems of the poverty groups around them. The settlements replied that they lacked the wherewithal to take on such problems as youth unemployment. When the federal government, through the corporation, offered the resources they needed, the settlements moved speedily to assume the tasks offered to them.

The voluntary vocational agencies were involved in a trading of their accumulated skill for the financial and prestige rewards of taking on the new program. (In one instance, however, the rewards turned out to be illusory, for the agency invested some of its own resources in new plant and new staff only to find its contract with the corporation terminated at the end of one year. The agency felt it had given far more than it had received in the exchange.)

The federal government, through OMAT and OJD, was interested in developing at the local level new techniques and arrangements for coping with a social problem. It was able *within limits* to exploit the power to dispense funds and to use that influence to define tasks and determine at least some of the agencies that would perform them. But its power was circumscribed by the legal rights and responsibilities of the state agencies and by the political price that the corporation had

had to pay for its leadership position among community agencies. Thus some limitations on the "federal funds" strategy for organizational change were discovered.

At the community level the corporation, as the innovator and the conduit for federal funds, was able to utilize the inducement of new resources and prestige and occasionally direct political pressure to persuade other agencies to take on new roles and alter their ways of doing business. The outcome was the coordination of agencies in a new program that was not entirely satisfactory to any of the organizations, but that was sufficiently rewarding to bring them into a new service configuration designed to deal with the problems of youth unemployment.

QUESTIONS FOR DISCUSSION

1. What are the relative advantages and disadvantages of attempting to achieve organizational change in a community by funding a new planning and coordinating agency as compared with funding an already established agency?

2. Should the corporation have operated any program components or contracted all with existing agencies?

3. To what extent were the federal guidelines helpful or harmful in determining the participation of local agencies?

4. Did the participating agencies view the entire program as a device for helping them to extend their services or as a device to stimulate them to change?

5. Do you agree or disagree with the allocation of program components to the specific agencies selected?

Employment Service Personnel in a Private Agency: Who Supervises Out-Stationed Civil Service Employees?

An experimental youth-work agency requested the employment service in its state to out-station a number of placement counselors at its offices in an effort to provide unemployed youth with the advantages of experienced ES personnel and ES job orders. The agency also hoped to encourage organizational change in the ES by exposing some of its personnel to the new policies and procedures in the youth employment field with which it was experimenting.

The issue of whether the agency or the ES would supervise the out-stationed counselors immediately arose, with each party asking for full control. A compromise was reached leaving the ES with supervisory authority but with its counselors serving only those youth ineligible for the agency's total services. But this compromise resulted in a subsequent decision by the ES to reduce the number of its out-stationed counselors because they were carrying inadequate numbers of clients.

The conflict reflected the differing organizational interests of the ES, which received its federal operating funds based upon the number of its verified job placements and other activities, and those of the agency, which was especially concerned with provision of intensive services to youth prior to placement. Different personnel policies and practices also contributed to the conflict, which was never completely resolved.

BACKGROUND

The original operating proposal submitted for federal funding in 1962 by a private, nonprofit youth-work agency in a large city provided for the out-stationing in its job placement unit of staff members of the state employment service. The program's planners believed that, because of the ES's experience in making placements and its access to large numbers of job orders from employers throughout the city, its placement counselors would be especially effective in referring job-ready youth to regular employment opportunities. At the same time, the youth-work agency's planners hoped that the ES counselors stationed in its offices would be exposed to some of the experimental client-oriented techniques they were innovating and that this experience might suggest modifications in what, they believed, were the more traditional employer-oriented policies of the ES.

The state employment service, for its part, had established its own youth employment program two years earlier in response to public concern that growing youth unemployment was leading to higher rates of juvenile delinquency. Although the ES had provided some specialized service to young workers since the early 1930s, these were not specifically directed toward out-of-school, out-of-work youth until 1960. In that year, with its own funds, it began out-stationing youth counselors in disadvantaged and ghetto areas of the city, utilizing facilities of such agencies as settlement houses, YMCAs, and housing projects, to refer youth to available part- and full-time jobs.

In their initial request for federal funds, the planners of youth-work agency proposed that the special youth services office of the ES provide the out-stationed placement counselors. They did not, however, discuss this proposal with the ES before submitting it, because they believed the ES would agree to participate in the job placement activities of the agency as part of its continuing public responsibility in the employment field. They further assumed the ES would absorb the cost of its out-stationed personnel from its regular budget, so that no funds were requested in its proposal for this purpose.

The first direct contact between the agency and the ES came in August, 1962, after the youth-work agency had been funded. The agency's youth-work director requested a meeting with the ES official responsible for youth employment services. There he informed the ES representative of the program proposal and requested that a total of eight ES placement counselors be assigned to the agency when its placement activities became fully operational. The ES representative received the impression that the ES staff would have full responsibility for all job placement activities of the youth-work program.

He pointed out that the youth employment service of the ES was currently out-stationing counselors at 32 different agencies in the city serving disadvantaged youth, including one center (a settlement house) located in the slum area to be served by the youth-work agency. Because the ES had these commitments, and because the agency was unable to pay for the additional personnel requested, the ES representative stated that eight placement counselors could not be assigned. Under the existing budgetary restrictions, he told the agency representative, only one ES counselor could be out-stationed in his program. But the youth-work director suggested that, with the approval of the settlement house, the counselor assigned to it might be transferred to the agency, giving it a total of two. The settlement house gave its approval to the transfer, and by the fall of 1962 the two ES counselors were stationed at the new agency. One of them attended the agency's own staff training and orientation course.

IDENTIFICATION OF THE PROBLEM

The initial ES impression that its out-stationed counselors would have complete control of the job placement activities of the agency was based on the agency's original request for eight full-time staff members. But when the ES asked the agency to clarify the extent of its control in view of the reduction in the number of counselors actually assigned, and to define their precise functions, it was told that the agency expected to exercise full control over all job placement and counseling activities provided in their program, including job development activities. Job placement, the agency said, was a major component of its comprehensive youth-work program and thus had to be fully coordinated with its training, counseling, and job development components.

The ES declined to accept this view for several reasons. First, full agency control of job placement activities implied supervisory authority over the out-stationed ES counselors and, under ES staff regulations, its out-stationed personnel were required to remain under the supervision of their ES superiors. Such control was necessary, according to the ES view, to maintain certain ES policies and procedures such as nondiscrimination in job orders and the maintenance of confidentiality of job applicants' personal data.

But, perhaps more important, federal reporting standards for ES placements were very exacting. The ES could report as placements only those cases in which the ES had secured the job order from the employer, selected the applicant, referred the applicant, and verified that the applicant had begun work. If its own supervisors controlled the activities of its placement counselors, the ES would be able to report that its policies and procedures were indeed being followed. But if its out-stationed counselors were supervised by a private agency, the ES would be unable to report placements made by these counselors to the federal government. The number of such placements was at that time an important factor in federal budgetary evaluations of the efficiency of the state employment services.

Both the ES and the agency anticipated that the number of actual job placements would be low in relation to the total caseload of the agency, since it was serving only disadvantaged youth who needed intensive preplacement training and other supportive services.

The primary issue that arose, therefore, concerned who would supervise the out-stationed staff, but several secondary problems which affected staff morale also developed. For example, the salaries of the agency staff, some of whom were to perform similar functions, were generally higher than those of the ES staff, while their hours of work were often longer and less regular.

COPING WITH THE PROBLEM

A series of meetings was held between the director of the agency's youth-work program and ES representatives in an effort to resolve the conflict. The agency's representatives submitted a compromise decision after it became clear that neither his nor the ES's preference for complete control of the job placement activities would be mutually acceptable. The compromise proposed that the ES counselors would remain under the supervision of their ES superiors but that they

would advise only those youth who lived outside the demonstration
service area of the agency and who were therefore ineligible for comprehensive agency services. Eligible youth would continue to be coun-
seled by agency staff.

ES representatives agreed to the compromise proposal, but with
some reservations. In order to serve the large number of unemployed
youth in the city and report job placements, the ES program director
had to ensure the most efficient possible use of his staff. He expressed
some doubt whether the number of "ineligible" youth needing job
placement services in the agency's program would justify even a single
full-time ES counselor. The ES representative proposed, as an alternative, that ES counselors be withdrawn completely and that the
agency refer "ineligible" youth to existing ES offices in their home
areas.

The agency resisted this proposal because it would deny services of
the experienced ES placement counselors, with their special access to
city-wide job orders, to the program. In addition, through continued
staff interaction and joint participation in agency-operated in-service
training, it was hoped that the ES staff would become exposed to
broader and more intensive counseling techniques. The agency's
youth-work director therefore declined the ES proposal, while the ES
agreed to accept the compromise proposal, at least on a wait-and-see
basis.

After several months of operation, however, the ES supervisors became convinced that their previous misgivings were justified: not
enough "ineligible" youth were being referred to their ES placement
counselors to justify their time, when measured against the demands
of other youth in the city. In the middle of 1963, therefore, the ES
informed the agency that it could no longer afford to continue the
experimental arrangement and suggested two alternatives. Either the
agency would have to refer more youth to the ES counselors from
among its eligible caseload or one counselor would have to be withdrawn.

The agency's youth-work program chose the first alternative and the
ES counselors were assigned "eligible" youth in addition to their previous caseload. This decision meant that ES counselors would now be

required to provide intensive preplacement and follow-up counseling, in addition to the more restricted placement counseling which they had previously offered. And shortly thereafter, when a larger number of youth began coming into the agency program, the ES was asked to assign two to three additional counselors to job placement activities —all of whom would remain under ES supervision. The agency repeated this request on several occasions when the backlog of job-ready youth was especially large.

Once again the ES was faced with decisions on where its youth services counseling staff could be utilized most effectively to make the largest number of job placements. The continued growth of various youth-work programs in the city meant that additional private agencies had asked for and were continuing to request ES counselors, and the ES program director made a constant review of his outreach activities. Counselors were shifted in response to the opening of new centers and declining caseloads or closings of old ones, and still no funds were being made available from the private agencies for these personnel. After careful consideration, the ES was forced to turn down the agency's requests for raising the number of out-stationed counselors to more than two. Its directors decided that demands elsewhere were more pressing, and the only alternative, an increase in ES staff, was not possible because of budgetary restrictions.

CONSEQUENCES

The effect of the conflict over supervision and effectiveness on the ES counselors out-stationed at the agency was pronounced. As they came into daily contact with the agency counselors, they were exposed to different conceptions of youth-work program policies and practices (such as reduced emphasis on placements and increased emphasis on training and supportive services), as well as different salaries, working hours, and personnel practices. One ES counselor responded to these factors by resigning from the ES and joining the staff of the agency for a brief time.

Another specific problem arose over the policy concerning

the confidentiality of job orders. ES policy stated that the names of employers sending job orders to the ES could not be released to outside agencies, and the youth-work agency was so informed when it requested that the out-stationed ES counselors make their job orders available to agency counselors. The ES held that employers' names were confidential because other agencies might cooperate with employers on discriminatory hiring policies. But perhaps more important, the ES was aware that the number of job orders which it had was insufficient to serve all the youth requesting placement from ES personnel. Thus, while informing the agency that ES job orders would be open to any qualified youth it wished to refer, it insisted that these orders would be filled only by ES counselors under ES supervision. Only through this procedure could the ES be entitled to receive credit for job placements under federal policy.

On occasion, however, the ES counselors did make employers' job orders available to agency counselors on an informal basis because of their personal sympathy with their clients. This was done contrary to official ES policy, however. Because of further demands for its out-stationed placement counselors, the number assigned to the agency was reduced from two to one in June, 1967.

QUESTIONS FOR DISCUSSION

1. What were the major reasons both the ES and the agency wanted supervisory authority over the out-stationed ES counselors?

2. Do you agree with the compromise decision which differentiated responsibilities between ES and agency counselors?

3. In your view, was the ES policy of maintaining complete control over its job order file consistent with its policy decision to expand its services on an out-station basis?

4. Was the willingness of the ES to participate in the agency program an indication of its willingness to make organizational changes?

5. Were there alternative ways for the agency to ensure fuller ES participation in the youth-work program?

"New Wine in Old Bottles": A State Employment Service Assimilates CAUSE Trainees

꿲꿲

As part of a nationwide Department of Labor program to expand employment and training for disadvantaged youth (and, in the process, to change the employer orientation of the state employment services), a special summer training program entitled Counselor-Advisor University Summer Education (CAUSE) was conducted by a state university. The graduates of this course, selected from college students and graduates committed to joining the "war on poverty," were assigned to the ES's Youth Opportunity Centers (YOCs), the major component of the Department of Labor's program to reach out into the poor communities.

The ES of this state was faced with the problem of balancing its desire to expand its services against its interest in preserving the stability of its existing organization. When frictions were produced as CAUSE trainees and ES personnel came together in the new YOC, the ES directors made efforts to assimilate the new employees into the existing organization. These involved decisions to conduct special training, rotation to other offices of the ES and, finally, dispersal of the remaining CAUSE graduates to a variety of ES activities. Directors of the ES concluded that some relatively minor changes should be made in their procedures as a result of the new employees' suggestions, but that in general their efforts had resulted in the successful assimilation of the CAUSE trainees.

BACKGROUND

In June of 1964, the Secretary of Labor announced a nationwide crash program to recruit and train 2,000 "counselor aides" and "youth advisors" to assist in the operation of work programs for disadvantaged youth. The program, called CAUSE (Counselor-Advisor University Summer Education), was an effort to (1) demonstrate the commitment of the Labor Department to solving the problems of unemployed youth, an issue of growing concern in the nation; (2) produce organizational change in the state employment services' perceived orientation toward satisfying employers' hiring standards for highly employable workers; and (3) recruit a sizable number of highly motivated employees for the employment service committed to joining the war on poverty.

The recruitment drive netted about 22,000 applicants, of whom 3,500 were selected to fill the 2,100 openings in an eight-week summer preplacement training program. All candidates were to be either college graduates or more than twenty-one years old, with some background in counseling or related fields and unemployed at the time of selection. Intensive full-time training was provided by twenty universities across the country, with the corresponding state employment services participating.

In a western state, the state university conducted the training for twenty-five CAUSE recruits from July to September of 1964. The training director found that his group consisted of three different kinds of students: highly qualified persons for whom his curriculum was superfluous, non-college graduates for whom it was too advanced, and recent college graduates, comprising about 25 per cent of the group, for whom the program seemed to be appropriate.

In accordance with the Department of Labor's training design, the ES was responsible for about ten hours of the CAUSE curriculum. Included were lectures on the application-taking process, occupational titles, principles of classification, interviewing techniques, principles of order-taking and order-filling, local office procedures, employer relations, and the functions of the youth employment programs. In addition, the trainees were assigned field work experience in actually counseling two or three youth being served by the ES. Finally the trainees were given on-the-job experience through the ES in their professional, clerical, and sales office, and their service and industrial office. They were rated on their suitability for future employment by the supervisors of those offices.

The state employment service had been informed by the Department of Labor that graduates of the CAUSE training program should
be hired as regular ES employees and that they might be especially
appropriate for assignment to the proposed Youth Opportunity Centers of the employment services. These were special facilities to be
located near a community's poor districts which would reach out to
disadvantaged youth, refer them to jobs or training programs, and
provide ongoing counseling.

At least two major policy decisions regarding the ES's commitment
to the expansion of services to disadvantaged youth—the establishment of the CAUSE and the YOC programs—were made at the national level. The major problems which the state ES faced in implementing these policies were related to integrating the trainees into the
existing ES structure and coping with their impact on its policies and
procedures.

IDENTIFICATION OF THE PROBLEM

The first indication of conflict between personnel of the CAUSE
program and the ES appeared in a telegram sent by the director of the
state university's CAUSE program to the Secretary of Labor before the
two-month training period had been completed. The training director
strongly urged that the proposed national YOC program *not* be administered by the state employment services. Apparently he based this
conclusion on his experiences with ES personnel assigned to participate in the CAUSE program, who he believed reflected the ES's lack
of understanding and commitment to effective programs serving disadvantaged youth. "Do not put new wine into old bottles," the training director advised the Secretary.

The university's final report on the CAUSE program was more
specific concerning the training capability of ES personnel: "While
some representatives of the ES were highly enjoyable, we regret the
inclusion of a number of ES personnel who apparently viewed the
CAUSE program as a convenient 'dumping ground' for a number of
upper-level functionaries with whose Saturday mornings it knew not
what to do." The report charged the ES personnel had merely read
printed manuals to the trainees.

The ES on the other hand felt that indoctrination into ES methods and procedures was an important component of the CAUSE curriculum, because, after all, its graduates were to be employed by that agency. The ES also believed its personnel were better qualified to conduct this training than the university staff members. The university's report concluded: "It is further to be hoped that top-level ES personnel will refrain from telling us, at least by implication, that they consider us supernumeraries of the most useless and repugnant type." An ES supervisor, while praising the majority of the trainees as "highly motivated," suggested that "if this type of program was undertaken again, it would be well to give serious consideration to a better break-out of individuals in accordance with their academic background and the experiences which they have gained through participation in work involving this kind of knowledge." The implication seemed to be that better selection of the trainees could have been made.

In general the university CAUSE training program director thought it unlikely that the ES would be able to change its employer-orientated perspectives sufficiently to enable the CAUSE goals to be met, and he communicated these views to the trainees. Since the trainees were aware that their "mission" was to achieve organizational change within the ES, they graduated from the CAUSE program nonetheless, with (in the words of an ES official) "a driving need to change the ES; to redirect its activities; and to loosen the traditional established, institutionalized ES way of life."

The state ES, however, wished to integrate the CAUSE trainees into its own staff without "rocking the boat" too severely. Its top staff were not opposed to expanding ES services to disadvantaged youth through the establishment of YOCs and the hiring of CAUSE graduates but wished to maintain at the same time its primary function of serving employers and average job-seekers. Efforts to absorb the CAUSE trainees successfully while achieving both goals occupied the ES's attention over the next several months.

COPING WITH THE PROBLEM

After the CAUSE training was completed in September, 1964, the ES began selection of those graduates it wished to employ. One of the hopes expressed by the planners of the CAUSE program was that state civil service hiring requirements for ES staff personnel might be relaxed to permit mature CAUSE trainees who were not college graduates to be hired in professional and semiprofessional positions. In this state the civil service system refused to modify its requirement of a college degree for ES personnel. The ES, wishing to "maintain the quality of its staff," did not oppose this decision although some ES executives supported the hiring of non-college graduates. It did make one "concession," however, in hiring one CAUSE non-college graduate in a clerical position (after this employee completed his B.A. requirements, he was promoted to counselor at the YOC).

Because of this and other factors, only sixteen of the twenty-five CAUSE graduates were actually hired by the state employment service. Since neither the state civil service nor employment service wished to lower its educational standards, this CAUSE goal was not achieved.

Where to place the sixteen CAUSE graduates was the next question to confront the ES. The YOC facilities were not to be ready for several months after the completion of training, so the ES was faced with the alternative of placing the new employees in various areas of its existing program or continuing the training period. It emphasized the latter, partially because the ES hoped it could ease the process of assimilating the new and old employees by exposing the CAUSE graduates more thoroughly to the perspectives and routines of the ES. As an ES executive put it: "In some cases, personnel relations suffered as these "upstarts" made their efforts to change the attitudes of ES personnel. These were anxious and painful times."

To assist in the process of assimilation, a five-week training course was designed by the state civil service training director and the state director responsible for implementing the CAUSE program. The training took place at a private university and was devoted primarily to problems of mental retardation, "which seemed to fill a gap that the CAUSE training missed." This program included instruction by personnel from the state school for the mentally retarded, the state board of health, a university medical school, and the retardation specialist from the local school system. In addition, the new employees were assigned on a rotation basis to field work in local welfare, vocational rehabilitation, service and other community agencies that serve the mentally retarded, as well as to several ES offices. Although some of the CAUSE trainees appeared to resent the implication that training in work with the mentally retarded would better prepare them to counsel disadvantaged youth, the ES reported that the trainees became "starkly aware of bureaucratic processes" and that a "two way testing process about attitudes, biases and other interpersonnel traits were experienced by both the ES trainers and the new employees."

When this training period was over in early October, 1964, the CAUSE graduates were assigned to full-time work in either the professional, clerical and sales or the service and industrial local offices of the ES. Here the local office supervisors were faced with the first daily full-time working contact with the CAUSE trainees and frictions immediately became apparent. The new employees, according to an ES official, "constantly attempted to meet their need fostered by CAUSE training—to loosen the traditional, institutionalized way of life. Some ES personnel were just as determined to preserve the procedures with which they were acquainted."

For example, CAUSE graduates concentrated on their personal relationship with the client while ES personnel were critical of inadequate and poorly written job orders taken by CAUSE graduates. They in turn were critical of ES personnel who were interested in a "pretty" application rather than meeting the needs of the client. Reporting procedures were a serious problem for the YOC management and staff.

The CAUSE graduates continually urged: "Why worry about reporting? Let's concentrate on service to the applicant and to hell with the rest." Experienced ES personnel on the other hand were concerned with reporting procedures because they were eager to receive credit for the work that they were performing for both applicants and employers. Tensions between the two groups of employees became so high that the director of field operations for the ES, after consultation with the office managers, decided to hold several meetings with them and their supervisory staffs about this problem. A frank discussion of this conflict produced suggestions that some rotation of CAUSE trainees to other offices might be attempted, but not until selection of the YOC staff was completed.

The YOC facilities were finally completed in November, 1964, and thirteen of the sixteen CAUSE graduates were assigned to work there (the remaining three, at their own request to be near their homes, were assigned to other local ES offices). Besides the manager and the supervisory staff, nine existing ES professional personnel were transferred to the YOC office.

Among the first conflicts between the CAUSE-trained staff and the transferred ES staff occurred when procedures were planned for handling the applicants for YOC services. The CAUSE graduates favored more informal and personal discussion with the youngsters regarding their backgrounds and interests, whereas the experienced ES counselors tended to rely on standard questionnaires and established classification and referral procedures. In general the new employees viewed the YOC program from the perspective of service to disadvantaged youth, while the older staff members brought with them their view of the ES as an aid to employers.

In the words of an ES executive, "these attitudinal differences between the old and the new frequently became sharp and emotional." After several months of operation of the YOC, the office manager decided to hold regular weekly staff conferences in which such problems could be thrashed out. These conferences served to open discussions of personal and "housekeeping" problems of the center as well as attitudinal and procedural problems.

A second method of coping with the conflicts between the transferred ES staff and the CAUSE graduates was the exchange, through rotation, between some of the YOC staff and placement and claims office personnel. The purpose of this rotation, proposed earlier and supported by the YOC manager and the director of the state ES, was to acquaint the two groups of employees with their respective problems and demands, to facilitate the assimilation of the CAUSE employees, and to expose older personnel to some of the new approaches to clients being tried in the YOC.

The attempt did not succeed. One CAUSE graduate assigned to the placement office left the position after three months to return for an additional period of CAUSE training (the second CAUSE program conducted in 1965). He charged the placement office personnel with shunting him to a variety of fill-in tasks which removed him from full participation in the activities of the office. Among the older ES staff, at least one considered rotation to the YOC as "punishment" and an interruption of his professional work as a claims adjudicator. He was, according to an ES supervisor, "terribly negative, disappointed and disgusted about having to make the move."

Although some of those rotated adjusted well and did contribute to a better understanding of the different functions of the ES, another CAUSE graduate complained of assignment to "busy work" in the placement office. But more important many ES personnel with long tenure in their posts considered rotation a threat to their careers. Their continued and strong pressure and protests persuaded the state ES director to discontinue the effort after six months.

After about one year of operation of the YOC, seven of the original sixteen CAUSE graduates had left the ES. At that time, the YOC was absorbed in a new ES activity serving disadvantaged persons of all ages. The ES decided to give the nine remaining CAUSE graduates opportunities for promotion and exposure to other ES operations by dispersing most of them to other offices. Three were assigned to the center, two to the placement section of a local ES office, one as a youth counselor to another local office, one as intake counselor in yet another office, and one to counseling duties in a rural office. This dispersal, combined with a year of ES efforts to assimilate the CAUSE graduates, resolved most of the frictional problems between the new employees and the experienced ES staff.

CONSEQUENCES

Of the seven CAUSE trainees who left the ES, four left for other work, two returned to college, and one was terminated by the ES for "failure to make the adjustment to the YOC."

The efforts of the ES to "integrate" the CAUSE trainees through special training, meetings, and supervisory techniques, and finally dispersal in assignments were successful in "assimilating" them into the larger organization. An ES executive attributed the "loss of the trainee's original identity (as highly motivated persons committed to "shaking up" the traditional perspectives and procedures of the ES) to their "dispersal throughout the large organization."

Although the ES was able to preserve its fundamental identity while encouraging the CAUSE graduates to lose theirs, it did permit certain modifications of procedures as a result of the program. The staff meetings pioneered by the YOC center were encouraged elsewhere; brighter office furnishings, more informal dress, and use of the ES facilities after working hours were all favorably received after their initiation by CAUSE staff. In addition, less "over the shoulder" supervision of professional staff, also recommended by CAUSE trainees, was favorably considered.

QUESTIONS FOR DISCUSSION

1. Was it wise to recruit a selected group of highly motivated trainees for a program to be run by a very traditional and structured agency?

2. What were the advantages and disadvantages of having the training conducted by the university as compared with having it conducted by the ES?

3. What were the consequences of informing the trainees that "their mission was to achieve organizational charge"?

4. What did the subsequent five-week training course developed by the state civil service director suggest concerning his approach to problems of disadvantaged youth?

5. What is your view about the rotation method as a way of improving mutual understanding and reducing conflict?

6. Does the dispersal of the remaining nine CAUSE trainees reduce or increase the likelihood of their effecting organizational change?

Programed Learning within a Correctional Institution: Organizational Change through a Demonstration Project

꽃 꽃

A private research group wishing to demonstrate a new programed educational technique developed by its members approached a federal youth correctional institution and requested permission to test and demonstrate the technique with some of its deficient students. The research group had previously gathered some evidence of the effectiveness of the technique and now wanted to achieve its adoption in public school systems.

They selected a youth correctional institution as a demonstration site because it had a lesser investment in its existing educational system and would therefore be more receptive to change. The institutional staff became enthusiastic about the technique within several months of operation. But the researchers now saw the need for restructing the entire institution environment around the new technique and proposed its expansion. The institution's staff agreed, and a group of thirty student-inmates were selected to spend 24 hours a day in a building especially converted for the purpose of the demonstration project. At this point the goals of the researchers included encouraging organizational change in the institution's correctional environment in addition to effecting changes in the educational techniques of public schools.

BACKGROUND

The educational director of a private research agency had developed a programed teaching technique of whose merits he was convinced, and in late 1964 he planned a strategy to achieve its adoption in public schools. The technique was based on rewarding the learning of a variety of school subjects (math, English, etc.) by enabling students successful on a given program to use entertainment facilities (television lounges, jukebox, and recreation room) available at the school.

The researcher was doubtful whether adoption of the programed learning techniques could be achieved by demonstrating the technique in either a university or a school, or even the newly funded Job Corps. The universities, he believed, were overly committed to "professional" learning techniques and would not be responsive. The public schools, some of whom the researcher had approached, seemed to feel threatened, and none would permit him to demonstrate his technique in their schools. The Job Corps, while receptive, emphasized fast results with little measurement.

He therefore turned to an institution which appeared to have little vested interest in its educational system and in which he would have a greater degree of operational control—a correctional facility for youth operated by the federal government. Education was only part of a correctional institution's program, and initial discussions with the superintendent and concerned federal agencies convinced the researcher that the institution's staff would be eager to implement any new techniques that improved the effectiveness of their educational system. Agreement was reached in these preliminary meetings that a demonstration project would be established within the correctional institution, and that it would comprise fifteen students "judged as having the worst educational problems."

At the insistence of the researcher, the project would continue for only six months. The researcher believed that by then either the institutional staff would be convinced of the effectiveness of the new techniques and be interested in adapting them to the entire educa-

tional program or the demonstration would have failed in its objective. If it did fail, less time would be lost by the institution, the
student-inmates, and the researcher himself then would be so in a
long-term project.

The project was funded by two federal agencies in February, 1965,
for a six-month period. The fifteen student-inmates were selected by
the institution's education supervisor from among his "problem
cases," and included students removed from the existing school system
for poor personal and educational behavior. Programed education
began for these students on the basis of a 3½ hour day in a facility
specially designed for this purpose. The students were "paid" a given
number of points for passing a selected unit in a course with a grade
of 90 per cent, and up to two times the basic number of points for a
score of 100 per cent. No points were given for a performance of less
than 90 per cent.

The basic technique used to reinforce (or reward) educational
achievement was to make available a student lounge with television,
pinball machines, and a jukebox, which could be used by any student
paying a given number of points per hour. Initial points, necessary to
participants in the system, were earned through correct responses on
an introductory battery of academic tests. Thereafter the student's
income was derived from course work. No student was forced or even
required to study; he could sleep or, if he had the required number of
points, he could relax in the lounge.

After the first several months, the number of points which could be
earned was raised for some courses (such as math) and lowered for
others (such as elementary English) in an effort to encourage students
to complete more challenging work. A mail-order catalog was provided, and student "points" became exchangeable for pennies toward
purchase orders of personal items. Individual study booths were con-
structed to provide private facilities, available for "rental" by the
students.

After six months in the project, student academic averages, measured by the Stanford Achievement Test, rose by 1.45 years (in less
than half of the regular school year). The SAT was chosen to measure

results not because the researchers considered it accurate (they did not) but because the results would be more familiar and acceptable to public school officials.

IDENTIFICATION OF THE PROBLEM

The staff of the demonstration project, as well as the institutional administrative staff, seemed satisfied with the results of the six-month demonstration, although few of the institution's officials professed to understand its methodology fully. Furthermore some of the educational staff of the institution questioned whether the original fifteen students accurately represented the total target population.

In an effort to involve the institutional staff in the project more fully, training courses were developed as part of a continued and expanded demonstration project, and the institution staff agreed to assign four teachers and five correctional officers from its existing staff to such participation and training. The researchers also proposed that the demonstration project be expanded from the original fifteen to thirty students, and that the additional fifteen would be selected to represent the educational levels, types of offenses, lengths of sentence, and family, racial, and geographic backgrounds of the institutional population.

But the primary problem facing the researchers was the absence of a supportive environment for the students in the programed education demonstration project. During the first six months the fifteen students spent only 3½ hours of the day in the demonstration program and then returned to the institution's regular residence facilities for the remainder of the day and night. The researchers believed that by establishing a total 24-hour living, working, studying, relaxing, and sleeping environment in which all normal activities could be conducted within the reinforcement system originally established for the educational demonstration, the general behavior of the students could also be improved.

At this point, a significant shift took place in the goals of the researchers. Originally interested in demonstrating the effectiveness of programed learning techniques for the purpose of influencing public schools, they now saw an opportunity to effect organizational change within the correctional institution itself. So while expansion of the original short-term project from part-time control of the students' educational program, to full-time control over their living environment was formally termed an effort to enhance the educational results of the short-term project, the researchers now became interested in demonstrating the effectiveness of the reinforcement technique for the total correctional environment.

COPING WITH THE PROBLEM

The benefits of the system included a potential reduction in the number of correctional officers required to control the students, whose behavioral problems were reduced by the new environment. In addition programed teaching techniques required fewer teachers than did the conventional classroom system.

Another tangible benefit for the institutional staff members was the growing recognition and publicity they were receiving from both correctional and educational agencies at the federal level and in other states. Such recognition enhanced their professional status and, as such, was an important factor in their receptivity to organizational change.

The institutional staff, already favorably impressed by the original demonstration, saw in the expanded demonstration the possibility of reducing behavior problems and achieving a better record for the institution as an innovator. The staff proposed, however, that if the demonstration were expanded to bring thirty of their inmates into an environment controlled by an outside group, the entire project should be supervised by a steering committee made up primarily of the institutional staff.

The researchers quickly agreed, since their strategy of achieving their new goal for organizational change depended on convincing the directors of the institution that change would benefit both the institution and the inmates. At no time did the researchers criticize the existing system; they hoped the new technique would commend itself through its demonstrated effectiveness. Thus, a steering committee was established, composed of the superintendent, the assistant superintendent, the captain of the guards, the directors of education and of classification and parole, and the director of the research project.

In an effort to involve further the existing institutional staff in the operation of the expanded demonstration project, the researchers proposed the project staff include, on a full- or part-time basis, seventeen institutional staff members including the five correctional officers and four teachers previously included in the staff training program. An additional reason for involving institutional staff members and directors was the researchers' knowledge that a new correctional facility was being planned to replace the present one. They therefore anticipated that if the staff members were thoroughly convinced of the desirability of change, they might ask that their new physical facilities be designed to incorporate the reinforcement environment.

The expanded demonstration project was funded in March, 1966, for one year. The institution made available one of its residence halls to house the demonstration program, and its facilities included study, recreation, living, kitchen, and dining areas. The rewards system for educational achievement was expanded from recreation facilities and purchases to include private rooms, better meals, personal clothing, and weekend (or longer) furloughs for those students with sufficient points earned from their studies and social behavior. Those without "money" had a dormitory-like room, standard institutional food and clothing, and no recreational privileges. Students not interested in educational achievement and thus not earning "money" were known as "living on relief."

The steering committee met weekly, and it was this situation that the demonstration project director utilized to suggest to the institutional staff the need for restructuring the correctional system. He introduced reports of the rising level of SAT achievement among the students, but without comparing it to that of the students in the existing educational system because he was confident the institutional staff would draw their own comparisons. After the expanded program began, the researcher was invited to attend the superintendent's executive staff meetings, where problems of the rest of the institution, not involved in the demonstration project, were discussed and solutions recommended.

This invitation signaled the superintendent's interest in restructuring the institution's entire environment along the lines demonstrated by the expanded project. He and his staff stated that comparison of the behavioral and educational achievements of the thirty students in the demonstration project and the rest of the institution's students clearly showed the benefits, both to the students and to the institution, of the new environment. The next logical step, he proposed, would be to adopt at least the educational techniques to the entire institution and, at a future time, to the new facility then being planned.

By the middle of 1966, then, the researchers began to withdraw gradually from the day-to-day operations of the demonstration project, leaving program operation to the institutional staff assigned for training. The director of the project cautioned the superintendent that he should not move too quickly in changing his existing procedures since some of the techniques required modification before they could be applied to a larger population. For example, results had to be measured carefully before definite conclusions could be drawn on how to adapt the new environment to the entire correctional institution.

CONSEQUENCES

A third phase of the project was being developed by the institution and the researchers in early 1967. It would involve the conversion of the correctional institution's total academic and vocational curriculum from its previous form to that demonstrated as being effective by the second phase of the demonstration project. The conversion had been approved by the federal agency responsible for the administra-

tion of the institution, which specified that its final form be determined prior to the institution's expected move to new physical facilities in the winter of 1967–68. The policy-making body for this project
would comprise the members of the second phase's steering committee,
and money was to be made available from the federal agency's own
funds.

While the change agreed to by the institution and its parent federal
agency was limited to the educational aspects of the demonstration
project, its expansion to include the total living environment was to
be discussed in the future.

QUESTIONS FOR DISCUSSION

1. Do you agree with the researchers' decision to shift their goal to promot-
ing organizational change in the correctional institution, or should they
have continued to test and refine their methodology?

2. What would you expect to be the problems which could arise when the
techniques demonstrated with the small group are implemented in a large-
scale program?

3. What could have happened if the successful education techniques had
required more correctional and educational staff?

4. What were the differing goals of the researchers and the institution?

5. What accounted for the institution's extreme receptivity to the new techniques?

Relaxing Host Agency Controls over a
Work-Training Program

A youth-work agency approached an urban general hospital to propose that a small number of disadvantaged youth be trained as nurses
and dietary aides through an experimental program. The agency's

goal was to demonstrate that such youth could be successfully trained and placed in health service occupations and thereby open new employment opportunities for them in the city.

The hospital administrators agreed to the proposal but insisted on maintaining complete control of all aspects of the training. Because they had strong reservations about the effect that employment of disadvantaged youth would have on the quality of service, the hospital administrators ruled out subsequent employment of the trainees in its own wards and largely limited their training to the performance of menial tasks.

The trainees, expecting a more substantial experience, refused to accept such "training." This crisis stimulated the youth-work agency, through a series of negotiations with the hospital, to persuade the host agency to loosen its controls of the training program. Through step-by-step demonstration that the training program and subsequent employment would not adversely affect hospital services, the agency gradually succeeded. Over a period of time the agency was permitted to conduct larger and more varied training in patient service occupations, and the hospital eventually agreed to hire many of the trainees.

BACKGROUND

In January, 1963, a private youth-work agency located in a racially mixed slum area of a large city contracted with a neighborhood general hospital to train a small number of disadvantaged young women as nurses and dietary aides. The agreement was negotiated in principle between the hospital and agency administrators, but responsibility for its implementation was delegated by the hospital to its personnel director. The youth-work agency assigned a staff member to the hospital training site as a coordinator, but the hospital administration retained major decision-making responsibility for implementation of the training program.

For a variety of reasons, the hospital's personnel director had strong reservations about the training program and insisted on maintaining close control over its operation. She saw an apparent contradiction between her responsibility for selecting nonprofessional personnel to serve the hospital's patients and a program that would permit disadvantaged youth, even under close supervision, to perform such functions. She also anticipated that the hospital's nonprofessional staff would view the trainees as potential threats to their jobs and that they would, through the hospital workers union, object to the trainees' subsequent employment at the hospital.

One factor contributing to the personnel director's attitude was the youth-work agency's public identification as a anti-juvenile delinquency project. In discussions with the agency, she expressed the fear that the trainees were being assigned to the hospital primarily for rehabilitation rather than for vocational training for hospital service employment.

For these reasons the hospital administration insisted that it retain complete operational control of the training program as a condition for cooperating with the youth-work agency. The hospital's personnel director, in preliminary discussions with the agency's hospital coordinator on implementing the program, translated the hospital's complete control into a series of specific program conditions. These clearly granted operational control of the training to the hospital (rather than the youth-work agency) and included the following:

1. Although the agency could select the youth referred to the hospital for training, the hospital could reject any one of them before his training began or terminate his training at any time. The hospital's personnel director explained that this condition would ensure that trainees met minimal hospital personnel requirements.

2. No trainees would be hired by the hospital as regular employees for a period of five years after completion of training. This condition would alleviate the alleged fears of the regular nonprofessional staff that the youngsters were being trained to replace them.

3. All trainees would serve two weeks in each of four divisions of the hospital. They would work in the housekeeping and laundry departments as well as in the nursing and dietary departments. The personnel director explained that rotation was required to give the trainees wider exposure to a variety of hospital work and permit them

to make a better vocational choice after completion of training, and to help fill the demand for housekeeping and laundry work, which was greater owing to a higher job turnover rate.

4. The youth-work agency would appoint a full-time liaison staff member who would be present at the hospital. Although the expressed purpose of this condition was to facilitate coordination of the program between the agency and the hospital, the agency representation was also to handle any disciplinary problems that might arise among the trainees.

5. No replacements would be permitted for any trainees who dropped out before completing the program. The hospital intended that this condition would result in referrals of highly motivated trainees to the program and ensure that trainees would complete the program in groups advancing at the same pace.

6. Trainees would be limited to females because the hospital believed disciplinary problems of males would be too difficult to control.

7. No youngsters with arrest records would be referred. The hospital cited existing personnel regulations for its regular staff as the reason for this condition.

The youth-work agency's administration accepted the hospital's control of the training program in principle because it agreed that only the hospital could actually conduct the training. While it expressed reservations about some of the specific conditions imposed by the hospital as an exercise of its overall control, it accepted them because there was no alternative if the program was to become operational. In early January, 1963, two weeks prior to the start of the training program, the youth-work agency hired its hospital coordinator, a former nurse with considerable experience in hospital procedures. Reviewing the conditions set by the hospital and accepted by the agency, the new hospital coordinator proposed that at least two of them be modified. The ban against hiring the trainees, she suggested, was a serious obstacle to the success of the program since the goal of the training was precisely employment in the nursing or dietary fields. She found that the hospital workers union had no objections to the eventual hiring of trainees and predicted that the staff of the hospital would similarly accept the trainees if the program was fully explained to them at meetings. The hospital personnel director rejected these proposals on her original grounds and informed the hospital staff that none of the trainees would be hired in that hospital.

The youth-work agency's hospital coordinator also anticipated difficulty with the condition that all trainees rotate outside the areas for which they were being trained, namely, the housekeeping and laundry departments. These jobs had low status and pay and involved primarily menial activities which the trainees might resent. The hospital's personnel director, citing her original reasons, insisted on this condition, however.

The agency administration did not fully support its hospital coordinator's recommendations, emphasizing that the hospital would not accept any trainees unless its control over the program was clear. Thus the training program opened at the hospital in late January, 1963, with eight female trainees beginning an eight-week program. Four began in the nursing and dietary departments and four in housekeeping and laundry work.

IDENTIFICATION OF THE PROBLEM

Before the first two weeks of training had been completed, the four trainees who had begun in the housekeeping and laundry components refused to report for work. They told the agency's hospital coordinator that they felt they were being exploited to perform menial functions in the hospital and that they were receiving no training in the areas promised, nurse's aide and dietary aide. Even before they refused to work, the personal appearance of the four trainees became unkempt and their work attitude was poor in comparison with that of the four whose first two-week training component was in nursing and dietary work.

COPING WITH THE PROBLEM

The agency's coordinator first discussed the problem with the trainees at length, explaining the rotation principle and urging them to "stick it out" until the nursing and dietary components were scheduled. She told them that this was a new program and appealed to them to accept it in the "spirit" of the youth-work agency. Privately, the coordinator agreed with the objections of the trainees. Nevertheless, the four trainees dropped out of the training program before completion of the two months, as did one of the other four trainees. Only three trainees, all of whom began in the nursing and dietary components, completed the program and were placed on jobs in other hospitals.

Before the end of the first group's training (March, 1963) the agency's hospital supervisor began new negotiations with the hospital's personnel director to alter some of the conditions to which she attributed the high dropout rate of the first trainee group. On the basis of the experience with rotation, the hospital agreed to decrease the laundry component from two weeks to one week and to increase the nursing component from two to three weeks. And by the beginning of the second group's training period, the hospital agreed to eliminate both the laundry and housekeeping components entirely and to increase the total training period from two to three months. By March, then, the program had evolved into a training experience exclusively for nurse's aides and dietary aides.

In addition to this "reform," the agency coordinator succeeded in opening the program to a few male trainees in the engineering (air conditioning, plumbing, and electrical maintenance) division of the hospital and in expanding the number of trainees from eight in the first group to fifteen, including two boys, in the second. This loosening of the original hospital conditions for the program was due in large part to the impression the first group had made upon the personnel director and the hospital training supervisors. Hesitant at first about what to expect from slum youth referred by a "juvenile delinquency" agency, the hospital staff apparently was impressed with the capacity and behavior of the first group of girls. In the words of one participant in the project, "The kids themselves really did the job of selling the program."

By the end of April, 1963, the second group was completing its three-month period of training. There were very few dropouts from this group, and the agency's hospital coordinator decided to attempt a "reform" of another hospital condition that, in her opinion, was a negative influence on the program. The ban on regular employment in the hospital was challenged in the following way:

The coordinator approached each supervisor who had worked with the trainees, expressed her gratitude for their work and cooperation with the group completing its training, and informed them that the youngsters would now be placed in regular employment in other hospitals. Many of the supervisors, having invested much time and effort in the training of the youngsters and believing that most of them would make reliable regular employees, indicated they would like to have most of the trainees hired on their staffs. Reminded that the hospital's training conditions prohibited this, the supervisors indicated they would ask that this policy be changed to permit the hospital to hire the trainees when they met employment needs and standards. Supervisors were reported to have approached both the hospital administration and personnel director with this proposal.

During the rest of 1963 relations between the hospital and youth-work agency continued to improve as the personnel director's confidence in the hospital coordinator's judgment grew. Although the personnel director occasionally rejected trainees referred by the youth-work agency without giving explicit reasons, the hospital coordinator noted one positive benefit of the rejections. They served as a check on the quality of the agency's screening procedure which, from the beginning of the program, had attempted to refer only those youngsters whose vocational counselors determined had a high probability of success in the hospital training program.

Despite the improved working relationships between the hospital's personnel director and the agency's coordinator, the former continued to express uneasiness that at least some aspect of the normal screening and hiring process was controlled by an "outside" agency. In an effort to demonstrate that the trainees referred by the agency were performing as well as the hospital's regular staff, the agency's coordinator suggested that turnover rates be compared between the two groups. But this test was never made by the personnel director.

In 1964, however, the hospital's fears about the trainees' performance after hiring had receded further. The personnel director agreed that youngsters should never be assigned to housekeeping work because experience indicated that all regular employees in this section were middle-aged or older. And when the agency's coordinator pointed out the legal distinction between juvenile and adult arrest records ("delinquents" and "youthful offenders" are adjudicated under civil rather than criminal procedures), the personnel director agreed to drop its ban on trainees with such records.

By late 1964, after almost two years of experience with the program, the agency's hospital coordinator proposed to the personnel director that the training be expanded to other areas in an effort to upgrade job opportunities. The personnel director agreed to include clerical training in the out-patient clinics and, in 1965, to expand to the records room and laboratories (clerical only), central services (packaging of sterile equipment), and shipping and receiving. However, the personnel director refused to permit training for laboratory or operating-room technician, stating that these positions were reserved for upgrading of regular employees.

CONSEQUENCES

Within three years of the establishment of the hospital training program, the seven major conditions through which the hospital asserted its control over the program were all modified, and four were completely rescinded.

1. *Rejection of trainees.* While the hospital continued to assert this authority, in practice it accepted an increasing proportion of those referred by the agency as the program became established, and its rejections became informally subject to negotiation with the agency's coordinator.

2. *"No-hire" policy.* Rescinded. The hospital did hire a large proportion of trainees.

3. *Rotation between menial work and work for which youth had been recruited.* Rescinded. The hospital terminated training in menial work.

4. *Full-time liaison.* The agency coordinator was retained, but she was not required to spend all her time in the hospital.
5. *No replacements for dropouts.* Replacements permitted once a month for phasing into the program.
6. *Female trainees only.* Rescinded. Males permitted in program.
7. *No trainees with arrest records.* "Adjudicated delinquents" and "youthful offenders" (youth under nineteen tried in civil proceedings) permitted in program if otherwise qualified.

From the summer of 1963 to 1966, the hospital training program sponsored by the youth-work agency was expanded to five additional hospitals, and in early 1967 it was operating in a total of five (one hospital was dropped). In the hospital described in this case history, the number of trainees in each three-month "class" was averaging between 40 and 45 in eight hospital work areas.

QUESTIONS FOR DISCUSSION

1. Why did the hospital insist on having complete control over the training program?

2. Should the youth-work agency have accepted the specific operational conditions, especially the ban on hiring of the trainees?

3. For the training program's goal of training disadvantaged youth for nonprofessional hospital employment, what were the advantages and disadvantages of the hospital's veto power over the selection of trainees?

4. What were the techniques used by the youth-work agency to reduce or modify the hospital's original conditions?

5. Was the agency coordinator's decision to persuade the rebellious trainees to "stick it out" an effective way to (a) hold them in the program, (b) persuade the hospital to eliminate its rotation training principle?

6. If the agency's coordinator had pointed out the legal distinction between adult and juvenile arrest records during the initial negotiations for the training program, do you think that the hospital would have dropped its ban at that time?

PROBLEMS OF RESEARCH AND EVALUATION

雅雅雅 *Introduction to the Cases*

When a relatively large amount of new funds became available through federal legislation supporting both general anti-poverty programs and those directed more specifically at unemployed youth, federal officials began to demand more reliable and systematic data to help them decide to fund a local program initially, to refund it, or perhaps even more importantly, to defend their funding decisions when the programs would come under inevitable political attack. As a result the program guidelines developed by the federal agencies made it clear that sponsors of local programs would be expected to build into their final proposals evidence that they could support their programmatic decisions with "hard data." Such data were to demonstrate the existence of a sizable problem (i.e., poverty or youth unemployment), the characteristics of those affected by the problem, and the relationship of all these factors to the program which was to be funded. Further, the potential sponsors were expected to plan for some organized way in which they would be able to assess the effectiveness of their programs. Consequently, and frequently for the first time, operators of local programs found themselves attempting to cope with their needs for programmatic research for purposes of planning, operation, and evaluation. And in all these areas they found themselves making a variety of critical decisions.

PLANNING

During the planning period a sponsor frequently turned to a nearby university as the one resource in his community with the technical competence to compile the requisite "hard data" describing his community and the target population. Universities generally were responsive to such calls for help, but academic researchers who actually participated soon found themselves in unfamiliar organizational roles involving them in policy and program issues which went far beyond their expectations or their expertise. Some found (perhaps to their delight) that they were now in the political arena, negotiating with contending community groups whose approval was required before a formal proposal could be submitted, and negotiating with the federal funding agencies as well. The university researchers, because of their inexperience with action programs, tended to be unsure of what their appropriate role should be, an uncertainty compounded by the lack of relevant experience of those directing the total planning efforts. Nonetheless, however ambiguously, researchers and action personnel soon were to participate jointly in a planning process, which had important consequences not only for the eventual funding of a program but also upon longer-range decisions affecting the ongoing relationship between action and research staffs.

OPERATION

When programs shifted from planning to operation, researchers were often unprepared for the demands which their action counterparts made upon them. The program staff tended to view the researchers as resources to record, store, and disseminate data quickly so that needed program modifications could be made on the basis of this feedback. The researchers protested that this was not their central function and further that they had been allocated meager resources to meet the need for systematic data collection. Such data collection as could be performed was dependent upon the efforts of the program staff who had direct contact with clients and who actually performed the services which were to be recorded. In addition the needs for data collection were compounded by the researcher's desire to prepare himself for future unanticipated requests for information by establishing data collection systems which others viewed as excessively complete, cumbersome, and costly.

EVALUATION

As federal poverty programs faced public and legislative scrutiny and criticism, and had to compete for funds with new programs and agencies, they were called upon increasingly to justify their continuation by showing "results." To be sure, the "results" expected by the legislators, the federal agencies, or the public at large usually have been neither explicit nor realistic. Nonetheless local agencies felt this political pressure and attempted to produce some form of program evaluation. And it is here that the program operators and the researchers experienced their greatest difficulties.

Under any circumstances research on program effectiveness is extremely difficult to perform. In general such research requires that the program to be evaluated remain relatively constant during the period of evaluation so that meaningful data can be accumulated. On the other hand, program administrators want to make programmatic revisions as soon as they feel they are needed. The conflicting needs for stability and flexibility caused frequent organizational strains which on occasion ultimately produced efforts to conduct action research that was free of such constraints.

To make matters worse, researchers frequently came to believe that the program administrators viewed evaluation as a device to produce a favorable view of the current program in order to support its efforts to continue, and perhaps expand, its services. Under such circumstances it is not surprising to learn that scientific rigor on the part of researchers performing the evaluation was often neither demanded nor even wished. In sum, decision-making involving action and research raised a wide variety of policy, organizational, and methodological issues, some of which are illustrated by the cases in this chapter.

The first case describes a situation in which a research department found itself responding to essentially political rather than professional issues. Its role, at a time of crisis, was largely influenced by its participation during the initial plannng period when the researchers developed a commitment to the organization and its program strategies that went beyond research. The research department's vulnerability to organizational needs was also increased by its earlier decision to focus upon program research rather than more academic and longer-range evaluation studies. We see in this case how decision-making is influenced by organizational loyalties and not just professional roles. The response to an outside threat in the struggle for survival was shared by researcher and program administrator. One wonders, however, whether this problem would have been resolved differently if the research department had initially been placed under auspices separate from the action program (perhaps a university). But possibly the most significant issue illuminated in this case is that (since crisis is almost inevitable in these programs) ways need to be found to protect research functions so that appropriate and useful work can continue.

In the second case we see an example of the conflicting needs for hard data for purposes of program feedback as compared with longer-term evaluation. The program administrator's need to satisfy his consumer, the funding agency, was quite different from that of the researcher who saw himself making a more general and perhaps more theoretical contribution to knowledge. It is understandable that differing senses of urgency emerged and staffs differing in attitudes, background, and training were recruited. From these differences flowed feelings of mutual distrust and unresponsiveness.

Even if the program administrators had wanted to make a general contribution to knowledge they would have quickly realized that they ran the risk of diverting the already scarce time of program staff to research purposes and, even more seriously, of exposing the program to a negative evaluation which could have threatened its very existence. Since the two research products were so different, it is clear that, in this case, the differences were recognized and led to the decision to create two separate research systems. It might be interesting to speculate to what extent the new organizational form will solve the existing problems while at the same time creating new ones.

The third case differs somewhat from the others in this chapter. Here we are confronted not by the organized activities of a formal research department but rather by the use of outside consultants to provide operational feedback to administrators based upon direct program observation by experts. The case is particularly interesting in that we see a most dramatic conflict arise concerning both access to information and dissemination of information which, while always a problem between action and research, was exacerbated as a result of a poorly defined contractual agreement concerning the role and functions of the consultant. Although the prime contractor thought it was purchasing assistance in certain technical areas, in problem solving, and in feedback, it appears that the outside subcontractors really hoped to use their knowledge and role as a way of changing the character of the program. And these differences produced the almost inevitable ensuing conflict, one aspect of which raised the question of academic freedom.

In the fourth case we consider an example of an attempt to overcome the difficulties of conducting program evaluation within an action program by converting an existing service activity into one conducting a rigorous experiment. The difficulties encountered and the decisions made emerge clearly as the administrators coped with the conflicting commitments to providing service as compared with the commitment to safeguard an experimental design.

To be sure, this conflict arises in all situations in which a research design limits the provision of services, but that situation was further complicated in this case by the imposition of a controlled experiment on a program and a staff previously entirely committed to providing services. This case also describes a highly effective way (from a service standpoint) in which staff coped informally with research barriers to service and shows how these informal solutions became formalized. While there was general agreement on the need for systematic research, the major question is whether it can be conducted within the framework of existing programs or whether it would be wiser to create new agencies whose specific mission would be the conduct of such research.

In the final case we see an illustration of program research conducted by an outside group which apparently was completely free of constraints by an action program. The research objectives and methodology were quite clear. However, the researchers quickly learned that an action program can and does play a critical role in the conduct of research by controlling access to information. This case provides a fine example of the design decisions which researchers must make when they undertake evaluation before the ingredients of the action program have become clear. One might have suggested to these researchers that their design problems would have been simplified if they delayed their research design until after the programs were well underway; nevertheless, one can sympathize with their desire to launch the research on this new program as soon as possible to ensure the greatest possible utility of their findings while public interest was likely to remain high.

This case is instructive in that it requires us to examine the relative advantage of access to information provided through "in-house" research as compared with the greater objectivity which may be more likely in "outside" research. We also see illustrated the pervasive fears that many program administrators have of scrutiny of their programs by outsiders whose very objectivity may pose a threat. Here the purely methodological problems of research became enmeshed in complicated organizational and political issues.

Program Planning Demands on a Research Department: What Are Appropriate Functions?

ꔆ ꔆ

In the midst of a political conflict between the administration of a comprehensive anti-poverty agency and a municipal government, the program's executive director asked his research director to draw up a proposal describing the agency's future programs. The research director believed that fulfilling this request required activities functionally inappropriate for a research department. He viewed program design as the responsibility of the program operating staff and agency administration.

The research director was also aware that the request was made in response to political pressure from the municipal government. He also believed that the actual content of the program proposal was essentially irrelevant to the outcome of the political conflict, which was based primarily on an agency administrator's unacceptability to the local government. Nevertheless, since he understood that it was possible that continuation of the agency's operations depended on his assistance in the program planning, the research director agreed to the request after considering a series of alternative decisions. The effect was a halt of much of the research department's normal operations, a deterioration in the relations between the agency's research and program staffs, and indirectly the eventual dissolution of the research staff.

BACKGROUND

The research staff of a private, comprehensive anti-poverty agency serving a racial ghetto area of a large city was recruited during the planning phase of the program in the fall of 1962. For more than a year a group of these research workers assisted in the collection of socioeconomic data on the potential target area to be served by the agency. Their role was confined to the collection and interpretation of data which was then turned over to the planning staff for development into program proposals. The new agency's program was funded by several federal departments and began operations about the middle of 1964.

Although the original grant proposal described the role of the agency's 12-person research department as both short- and long-range evaluation, the research director and his staff placed great emphasis on operational research and program feedback. They suggested soon after operations began that the long-range program evaluations be contracted to outside university investigators. (As examples of these different research perspectives, studies of staff functions and job descriptions, techniques of youth recruitment and the establishment of a central data bank were viewed as operational, or program, research, while long-term follow-up of trainees who left the program or a study of the effect of their participation in the youth-work program on their families were considered evaluative research). The research staff collected baseline survey data for long-range evaluation of the program, developed a clientele accounting system, and conducted several small studies.

The research director decided to focus on operational research for several reasons. First, a prominent researcher had left the agency amidst public controversy which tended to reduce the "credibility" and "objectivity" of long-run research conducted by the agency itself. Second, the research director believed that program feedback was a more immediate concern for the new agency and, third, that potential conflicts between the program and research staffs might be avoided if evaluative research were performed "out of the house."

For all these reasons the research director believed that the most effective evaluative research could be done by outside research groups and specifically recommended a particular university for this purpose to the agency's executive director, who agreed in principle with the research director's suggestion.

But when the agency's board of directors discussed this recommendation, the members hesitated and postponed a decision. Many board members were apparently uneasy about outside program evaluations because of their fear that critical findings, if made public, could adversely affect the agency. They inquired closely into the background and orientation of the prospective research groups and commented negatively about the suggested university, which had a history of poor relations with the community served by the agency. The program staff, on the other hand, welcomed outside evaluation because of their hope that some of the prestige of the university research group might "rub off" on their programs and because it might benefit the program's operations.

The board of directors continued to defer any decision on a research contract with any outside group until October, 1965, when the entire question became moot. As a result of charges of fiscal mismanagement, federal funding agencies suddenly withdrew authority from the anti-poverty agency to spend new funds and also established very tight control over the agency's previous money obligations. The program was permitted to continue its service operations. Although the government agencies acted in response to alleged fiscal irregularities, their action was also due to pressure from the municipal government for closer control of the local anti-poverty programs.

Basically, the conflicts between the municipal government and the program developed because the city administration feared that several already existing community-based anti-poverty agencies were threatening to become independent centers of political power. The federal action in freezing funds was demoralizing for many of the program and research staff members. Program activities slowed, and, as one participant described it, "Everyone sat around—there was nothing happening."

Shortly thereafter, the municipal government indicated that a financial thaw could be speeded if the agency would produce a well-developed proposal describing its future programs. (The federal funding agencies were expected to follow the city's recommendations in this matter). But the agency's staff strongly believed that this request was made to disguise the city's real demand: the removal of the agency's executive director in return for ending the freeze on funds.

While the manifest request was: "Give us an adequate program proposal and you'll have the money," many of the agency's staff considered this as a "cover" while the city government carried on behind-the-scenes negotiations. Until the agency executive was replaced, they predicted, the city would reject a series of proposals as "inadequate" or "unclear" or would ask for revisions.

Nevertheless the agency's director fulfilled his official role and appointed a task force made up of program staff to develop the requested proposal in early 1966. The resulting document, delivered to the municipal government shortly thereafter, was rejected as "inadequate" in March, 1966, and a new one was requested. The agency staff believed that the rejection was made because the executive still retained his position in the program and that therefore the actual city demand had not been met.

IDENTIFICATION OF THE PROBLEM

Immediately following the city's rejection of the agency's program proposal, the executive called the research director to his office and told him: "We need a program statement for the next year, and you and your staff are the only people we have who can draw it up." The administrator's motivation for this request was based on the several considerations: (1) The research staff had contributed the original successful proposal that led to the funding of the program; (2) the research staff would probably be viewed by the municipal government as more "objective," thus enhancing the possibility of acceptance of the proposal; and (3) since the program staff's earlier proposal had already been rejected, there was no other appropriate group within the agency able to prepare a suitable proposal.

COPING WITH THE PROBLEM

The research director's immediate reaction to the request was to protest that he and his staff were not program designers and that it was inappropriate, in view of their research responsibilities, to assume a program design function. His role, he said, should be limited to collecting and analyzing data on program operations and to making recommendations for planning purposes. He further asserted that he and his staff were not experienced in this area and were therefore not competent to draw up program proposals.

In addition to his stated reasons, the research director had other misgivings about the request. Both the agency executive and he were aware that the municipal government's demand for a new program proposal was not really central to the resolution of the underlying political conflict. Further, they believed that the proposal would be accepted or rejected on the basis of the outcome of the political struggle regardless of its programmatic merits. The research director felt that he was being asked to work not only in a capacity inappropriate to his function in the agency but also on a project that was, in the words of a participant, "at best a cover, at worst a fraud."

The research director saw four main alternatives open to him. He could (1) agree to work on the proposal, even though he did not consider it to be work which he and his staff were competent to perform; (2) reject the request of the executive, which might require his resignation from the agency; (3) propose that the work be contracted to an outside group, or (4) delay a decision.

The executive emphasized in response to the plea of "inappropriateness" that the situation was a critical one for the continued operation of the agency, and that therefore the differences between planning, service, and research functions had become blurred. On the issue of program competence he told the research director, "Maybe you're not competent, but you're the best we've got." Finally he said that the work could be completed within one week and that it would only temporarily divert the research staff from their more appropriate functions.

The third and fourth alternatives were rejected by the research director immediately. He believed it was unrealistic to expect that the proposal could be drawn up by an outside group because no funds were available for such purposes. And because the time factor was so crucial, according to the executive, he could not delay a decision on the request. But most important, he considered his primary role to be a member of an organization, responsible first to the agency rather than to a more general conception of the role of a research department. Since he did believe it was possible, (although unlikely) that the at least temporary survival of the agency depended on submitting an acceptable proposal to the municipal government, he decided he should not reject the executive's request.

Before the meeting was over, then, the research director had agreed to prepare the proposal with members of his staff. His commitment to the agency and its work outweighed his misgivings about both its appropriateness and its relevance to the real funding problem. He asked the executive to give him two weeks to draft a new program proposal.

CONSEQUENCES

Half of the 12-member research staff was immediately diverted from other duties to work on the proposal and shifted to "crisis operation," working day and night. But although a draft was completed within several weeks, the research director found that his planning duties were far from completed. In fact for the next year he and his staff agreed to develop redrafts of their proposal and to enter into direct negotiations with municipal officials, including those in the budget department. The research director thus gradually assumed a full-time political role as a negotiator between the agency and the local government departments concerned with anti-poverty operations. This role, however, was a "front" for other negotiations being conducted by others on the political level.

During this transformation of his role, the other work of the research department was impaired. Its staff drifted without supervision and leadership, and ongoing projects, including central data collection, ground to a halt. The research staff members involved in the negotiations became demoralized and believed the work was "meaningless" and "futile." Finally, the relations between the research and program staffs, once cordial and cooperative, deteriorated when the research planners began to function as budget inspectors and when they were required to review and amend program budgets, line by line, without even producing appropriations to keep program operations running smoothly. The program staff came to resent the research staff and refused to cooperate with it in this new role. When the research director left the agency in July, 1966, the research staff also drifted away. The federal funds were resumed after the executive resigned from the program, and the central political issue was thus resolved.

QUESTIONS FOR DISCUSSION

1. Was the request of the executive director appropriate or inappropriate? Why?

2. Do you agree or disagree with the research director's decision? Why?

3. To what extent did the research director's previous orientation influence his decision?

4. If the research director had refused, what would have been the consequence for research? The program? The agency?

5. Does this case suggest that research functions in action-research programs should be established and maintained under separate auspices and control?

Long-Term Research versus Program Feedback: A Youth-Work Program Establishes Its Own Research Section

An anti-poverty agency was established with a research department separate from its "action" departments which included a youth-work program. A conflict between the research department's data collection needs for its long-range research commitment and the differing needs of the youth-work program for program feedback data was identified in the early months of the program's operation when youth-work counselors refused to fill out the numerous data forms requested by the research department. At the same time the program director developed a need for program feedback data. This conflict between the needs and commitments of the research and action departments was temporarily resolved by a decision to utilize several members of the research staff on an informal basis to simplify the research department's data forms while at the same time helping to establish a central records unit for feedback data in the youth-work program.

But the conflict again arose when the youth-work program required extensive data for preparing progress reports to its federal funding agencies. Again the need was temporarily met by members of the research staff who decided individually to assist the program staff in this work. Eventually the problem of conflicting needs and commitments of the two departments was resolved by the agency's decision to establish a research unit within the youth-work program whose responsibility was solely to serve the program-oriented data collection and research needs of the action staff.

BACKGROUND

An experimental anti-poverty agency was established in a large city with a central research department having responsibility both for its own long-range evaluative research and for serving the data collection needs of all the agency's action programs, including its youth-work component. Within the agency's administrative structure, the research department was independent of and coordinate with the action departments because the agency planners believed that such independence would reduce the possibility of pressure from the operating departments and enhance the objectivity of the agency's research program.

Members of the research department were primarily oriented toward long-range "total impact" research from an academic perspective. They were concerned with testing a variety of theoretical assumptions about the causes of juvenile delinquency, the structure of teen-age gangs, and the social composition of the community being served. At the same time, the absence of explicit goals among the action programs of the agency during the early months of operation meant that specific data collection and program feedback needs were relatively undefined.

The combination of these factors caused the research department to seek as much information as possible about all aspects of the nature of the youth-work program's operations, without having a clear perspective on the use of the resulting data. For example, a wide variety of forms were distributed to the counseling staff of the youth-work program. Each time a counselor made a contact with a client, he was requested to fill out a different form describing the client and the nature of the contact in great detail. During these early months of operation, there was little discussion between the youth-work and research departments of the agency concerning the data collection needs of the action program, and thus the information being gathered by the research department was not meeting the needs of the youth-work program.

IDENTIFICATION OF THE PROBLEM

Most members of the youth-work program staff were deeply committed to a client-oriented perspective and opposed to bureaucratic procedures and forms of organization. Thus, when requested by the research department to fill out a large number of client contact and other forms asking for what seemed like a large amount of unnecessary and even irrelevant information, they became indignant. The vocational counselors, from whom most of the forms were requested, strongly resented the time and energy required to complete them, especially when, as in the early months of the program, quick service to the disadvantaged youth of the community was their primary goal. They believed the research department was imposing a bureaucratic system on their program that diverted them from that goal.

Several months after the program began operation, many of youth-work counselors participated in a "revolt" against the forms requested by the research department—they refused to fill them out. They chose this method to dramatize their protest against a data collection system that to them seemed to serve only the academic and theoretical orientation of the researchers and to divert their efforts from serving their clients.

At about the same time the youth-work director began to formulate the data collection needs of his program. He concluded that the type of program feedback information he would require for evaluation of his operations, which centered on the actual experiences of the youth in training programs and later in the labor market, was quite different from the broader sociological data needed by the research department. He therefore had to resolve a conflict between the data collection needs of the autonomous research department oriented toward basic theoretical research and his own service-oriented program staff whose data collection needs were more closely related to feedback from the program's operations. This problem had manifested itself through the alienation of the program's counseling staff to the extent that they "struck" against the large number of forms requested by the research department and the lack of continuous feedback data from the research department required by the program staff to assess its procedures properly and make necessary program modifications.

COPING WITH THE PROBLEM

The first attempt to solve these problems was the youth-work program director's request to several individual members of the research staff for a revision of their data collection methods. He asked these researchers to reduce the numerous forms to a single form that could be completed by the program staff in a relatively short time. The research staff then agreed to design a simple checklist to replace the widely resented client contact forms. The "strike" of the counselors was ended when this simplified checklist was put into use.

To meet the needs for program feedback data meanwhile, the researchers helped establish a central records unit in the youth-work program by bringing together in one location several types of existing records (such as federal forms, time cards, client records, etc.) that had previously accumulated in different locations at the program's offices. This centralization of records satisfied the immediate needs of the program operators for feedback data and further reduced the conflict between the differing needs of the research and program components of the agency.

But while these informal and ad hoc arrangements resolved the two initial manifestations of the conflict, they did not prevent similar problems from arising in different forms. About a year after the program had begun operations, several progress reports required by federal departments providing the agency's funds came due. Still without their own data collection staff, the youth-work program director again asked the same members of the research staff to assist in the preparation of these reports by providing summarized data from the central records unit.

The researchers agreed to do so, since they had become personally sympathetic to the needs of the program staff as a result of their earlier participation in solving the original problems of conflicting needs. However, they had become increasingly aware of their role as members of the research department, which had different interests and needs in the area of data collection. They expressed the fear that the data they were being asked to provide might be interpreted by the program staff as a means of impressing the federal funding agencies, and thus they perceived a potential conflict between their responsibility to "objective" research demands and the "practical" needs of the youth-work program.

For example, they realized it was possible to make different definitions of "favorable" and "unfavorable" outcomes of the program's vocational training efforts, and an analysis of such outcomes was an important component of the progress reports required by the federal agencies. A trainee who was recorded as having left the training program for what the youth stated was a "regular job" would usually have been accepted by the program staff without further questioning as a "favorable" outcome.

A researcher, however, might have preferred to investigate at least a sample of such trainees in order to determine whether the youngsters had actually found such employment or whether they had simply wanted to leave the program and had told their counselors they were regularly employed to avoid efforts to persuade them to stay in the training program. Several such areas of potential conflict between data collection needs of autonomous research and action departments were identified before the actual preparation of the agency's progress reports to the federal agencies.

Although, as one of the researchers put it, "a really hard-nosed research worker would have flatly refused" to assist in the preparation of the progress reports of the youth-work program, the members of the agency's research department agreed to the program director's request. They did so despite certain reservations about the appropriateness of their role as "objective" researchers because they became more deeply committed to the success of the program. In short their original orientation and commitment to the long-range research interests of the autonomous research department had shifted as a result of their informal assistance to the youth-work program staff in resolving the initial problems of data collection. They had developed personal commitments closer to client-oriented goals of the "action" department of the agency than to long-range interests of the research department.

CONSEQUENCES

Following the researchers' participation in the preparation of the youth-work program's progress reports to the federal funding agencies, the director of the youth-work program sought a permanent resolution of the conflict between the different data collection and research needs of the agency's autonomous research and action departments. He therefore proposed that the agency's administration establish a research unit as an integral part of the youth-work program. Its members would be directly responsible to the program's director and in all functional respects, including salary, would be members of the action staff. Their major responsibilities would be data collection relative to the youth-work program's recruitment, training, placement, and all other activities as well as occasional research projects in selected areas of program feedback. Unlike members of the autonomous agency research department, the orientation of members of the action program's research staff would be to provide service to the action program and not to the long-range evaluative research of the agency as a whole.

The agency's administration agreed to this proposal, and the youth-work program established its own research section directed by the same former member of the research department that had informally assisted the program director in the early months of operation. Some misgivings were expressed by the agency's research department, some of whose members continued to uphold the original rationale for the separate and autonomous research department—that the objectivity of its work would be enhanced because of its sole commitment. The question whether a single research department can meet both the long-range evaluative needs and the program feedback needs of a large agency was, however, not resolved.

QUESTIONS FOR DISCUSSION

1. How could the research department have tried to gain the support of the youth-work program's staff for their data collection needs?

2. Do you agree with the decision to establish a research department independent of the action departments of the agency?

3. Can you see any alternatives to the eventual decision to form a research unit within the youth-work program?

4. Could the original conflict between the different data collection needs of the research and action departments of the agency have been resolved without the existence of researchers personally sympathetic to the needs and goals of the youth-work program?

The Role of the Consultant: Conflict
in a Job Corps Center

꿋꿋

A university faculty group, after it had declined a federal agency request to submit a proposal for operation of a Job Corps center, was asked to provide consultative services to a corporation which accepted the contract. The subcontract between the university and the corporation provided for a wide variety of consultative services and was signed before the first group of trainees entered the center. But a difference of view between the university consultants and the administration of the center soon became evident.

The university consultants viewed their role as that of participants in the policy-making process of the center, while the corporation viewed it as that of advisers to "middle-range" program directors. This fundamental difference over their role also reflected important differences over a broad range of operational questions, and these differences were eventually expressed in a lengthy report by the consultants to the center director. When this report was made public, the conflict between the corporation and the university consultants became so intense that the consultants recommended to the university that the contract not be renewed.

BACKGROUND

In April, 1964, the President's Task Force on Poverty, engaged in studies and recommendations that later became the basis of the Economic Opportunity Act of 1964, asked the urban studies center of a state-supported university to submit a conceptual and operational plan for a major residential Job Corps center for males to be located within the same state. The university assumed it was asked to make this proposal because of its proximity to the base and because the Task Force intended that the federal government would eventually award contracts to academic institutions for operating residential training.

The university formed an interdisciplinary committee, recruited consultants, and drew up a proposal which was presented to the President's Task Force in the summer of 1964. The document was not a contract proposal. It did not offer the services of the university as the operator of the proposed residential youth-work center, but rather was a model which the university indicated it could develop into a formal proposal if the model met the Task Force's requirements. The model projected a small (500 enrollees) experimental center which could be expanded on the basis of demonstrated effectiveness with the first group of enrollees. The meeting ended in disagreement between the university and the Task Force primarily over the size of the proposed center (the Task Force preferred a larger center with 5,000 trainees) with the result that the university representative recommended that the university not prepare a formal bid on the project.

Perhaps because of its disagreement with the university over the size and scope of the initial residential program and its desire to involve private enterprise in the war on poverty, the group of government planners decided that private corporations should be approached as prime contractors for the centers.

In any case, the Task Force turned to one large corporation's subsidiary, which had just completed a major defense system and had a large training unit formed for that project. The corporation submitted a proposal for operating the proposed Job Corps center in the fall of 1964 which was quickly accepted in principle by the OEO. However, it was understood by the university consultants that the OEO attached a condition to the final letting of the contract: namely, that the corporation subcontract with an academic institution for consultative services. Later in the fall the OEO informally approached the university to inquire whether any of its divisions would be interested in such a subcontract. Three units of the university expressed interest.

Meetings between the corporation and the university were held during the winter of 1964, and a proposal was developed for submission to the corporation. Final agreement and revision of the proposal were made at two meetings in December, 1964, between the two parties held under the auspices of the OEO. At the last meeting after agreement on the subcontract proposal was reached, the corporation and the OEO signed the prime contract for operation of the Job Corps center. The university and the corporation signed the subcontract on January 1, 1965.

The corporation's contract with OEO included a provision for the subcontract with the university for services as a consultant and "in any way which could aid and support the capacity of (the corporation)" to carry out its contract. The university's proposal, to which the corporation had agreed in December, defined these functions as: (1) the development and conduct of orientation programs for the Job Corps center's staff; (2) the development, in conjunction with the corporation, of a system for enrollee self-government; (3) the selection, adoption, and review of planned academic courses at the center; (4) development and conduct of an orientation program for counselors; (5) the assignment of university "teacher-practitioners" responsible to the center's counseling and vocational educational department heads; (6) the placement of graduate students from the university in the center for training.

The proposal described the general functions of the university consultants as "participation" in the service operations to which they were to be attached and the laying of groundwork for the graduate student training. The consultants would also "participate" in the ongoing operations and through staff development activities "contribute as appropriate to the enhancement of the effectiveness of the operation of his department."

The contract between the university and the corporation listed the following "areas of endeavor" in which the university's consultants would function, although these were specified as not inclusive: (1) consultation with the center's director in "developing plans, programs and objectives and in measuring the results of the learning experience for the Job Corpsmen"; (2) consultation with the corporation's professional staff in training methodology and group living; (3) design and evaluation of experiments for measuring the training results.

The contract also specified that all university personnel were "administratively responsible" to the university's resident coordinator, that its personnel were subject to the corporation's approval before assignment to the center, and that specific work tasks would be agreed on between the corporation's center director and the university's center coordinator.

Although most university personnel recruited or assigned to the Job Corps center participated in the development of the original university proposal (and thus assumed it outlined their responsibilities as consultants), they were not aware of the actual contents of the formal contract, which was signed by the corporation and a fiscal officer of the university.

IDENTIFICATION OF THE PROBLEM

In January, 1965, before the arrival of the first group of corpsmen, the Human Relations Commission of a nearby town asked the corporation for a discussion on the anticipated impact of the Job Corps center on future community relations. It specifically requested that a consultant on community relations from the university attend this meeting, together with the corporation officials. The officials disapproved of the invitation to the university consultant and declined to meet with him prior to the discussion with the town's Human Relations Commission, but the consultant nevertheless attended.

At the meeting the commission offered to explore the possibility of providing recreational, educational, and employment opportunities for Job Corps enrollees in the community while, in response, the corporation's representative stressed that such facilities were available on the center grounds. The university consultant emphasized the desirability of developing all possible channels of communication between the enrollees and the surrounding community to enhance socialization of the enrollees.

In discussions between the consultants and the corporation, the consultants were informed that the center officials had decided, in an effort to reduce possible tensions between the enrollees and nearby communities, that the center would be as self-sufficient in recreational facilities as possible and would attempt to hold the enrollees within its gates. Reflecting concern about possible tension with the nearby town, the center staff issued a written directive stating that all community relations would be handled by the corporation staff, who would utilize prepared texts in all press and public relations. These decisions, of which the consultants were not then aware, formed the basis for the corporation's position on the first community meeting. They also clearly identified a conflict between the center and university staffs regarding views on basic concepts of the center.

When the university consultants advised against the "self-containment" policy of the corporation and warned of its potentially serious consequences for the enrollees, they were informed that their role was limited to that of advisers to "middle-range program directors" below the policy-making level. Their consultation was to be on a wholly "technical" basis and must avoid all areas of public relations. While this decision was conveyed verbally, a subsequent written directive stated that all public release of information of data on the center would be distributed through the corporation public relations office.

The first group of sixty job corpsmen arrived at the center in February, 1965. At about the same time one university consultant (then director of the social work component but later coordinator of the consultants) met for the first time with the corporation's manager of the education, vocation, and avocation unit. While the consultant intended to discuss placement of the social work students in the program, the manager instead asked the consultant to draft a curriculum on sex education for the corpsmen. This apparent lack of understanding of the corporation/university relationship was first evident in this exchange.

The problem that emerged from subsequent discussions between corporation and university personnel on the placement of the graduate students was that the university staff of consultants was guided by the informal university proposal for the subcontract while the corporation was basing its understanding of the relationship on the formal contract itself. Although agreement was eventually reached on the placement of the students, the much more significant issue of differing views on operations and the consultative functions remained.

The fundamental problem was the differences of the consultants and the corporation on the nature of the consultants' role. The consultants saw themselves as participants in the policy-making process of the center's administration who could therefore disagree with the center's policies as they saw fit. The corporation on the other hand believed that the consultants should be available to advise administrators on problems selected by the administrators, and that therefore the framework of consultations was to be established wholly by the administrators. For example, the administrators might ask the consultants to advise them on the problems of what time the dormitory lights should be turned off at night, and they would expect the consultants to suggest a specific time. The consultants, however, might consider that it was unwise to establish a specified time for "lights out" and would therefore make efforts to change this policy decision rather than advise on the problem of implementing it.

COPING WITH THE PROBLEM

Within three months of the opening of the Job Corps center, the number of university consultants had grown to twenty. A series of issues arose between the corporation and the consultants concerning the availability of feedback data from the counseling and educational units and other statistical data. The corporation refused to make such data concerning dropout rates, absenteeism, rates of induction, and academic progress of the enrollees available, citing the OEO limitation on release of research information. The consultants attributed several additional problems to what they concluded was a "cost-accounting perspective" of the corporation. For example, in an effort to keep barracks full and reduce costs of space not fully utilized, the suggestions of the consultants for grouping enrollees by length of enrollment, readiness for employment, prior skills, etc., were not accepted.

By April, the relationship between the corporation and the university consultants became so strained that the corporation dispersed the consultants among the center's functional divisions according to the areas of their technical competence. Previously the consultants were reporting to the center's director of education, vocation, and avocation and had offices in a central location. Their dispersal was effected by ordering them to report to the center's various program division heads and physically dispersing their offices. The reason cited by the director for the change was a need to reduce his "span of control" —twenty consultants were too many to be reporting to him.

The consultants interpreted this action as further limiting their role. Because working conditions within the center were steadily deteriorating, they formed an ad hoc advisory committee which would offer their recommendations collectively to the corporation. Alarmed by their perception of the poor atmosphere for the enrollees and at the tension and lack of communication between themselves and the center staff, they wrote a comprehensive report giving their diagnosis of the center's operational problems and offering their recommendations. The 100-page report was presented to the center director, together with an invitation to discuss it, in late summer of 1965.

No reply was received from the director for six weeks, and in November a crisis occurred when a major newspaper obtained a copy of the consultant's report and published articles about the situation at the center. When reporters and television cameras descended on the center, the corporation again invoked the clause in the consultants' contract that forbade release of any data concerning the center without approval of the corporation. This directive was ignored by the consultants, who had, in any case, been unaware of the existence of that clause in the contract when they began their work.

The open conflict between the corporation and the university over differing concepts of Job Corps center operation attracted nationwide publicity which resulted in further aggravation of their working relationship. In February, 1966, the consultants charged the corporation had violated their academic freedom by asking the university president to invoke sanctions against them. The corporation took the position that the consultants had violated the terms of their contract by airing the dispute in public. The university president took no action on the corporation's request.

The consultants then asked the deans of the affected schools of the university to meet with the corporation's project director, who had responsibility for fulfillment of the Job Corps contract, and convey to him the seriousness of the situation. Two of the deans met with the director in February, 1966, and discussed the role of the consultants. The meeting resulted in agreement that the consultants should have more access to Job Corps center officials and that they should be permitted to play a more effective advisory role on policy questions. Immediately after this meeting, and for a subsequent period of two months, the consultants' coordinator was asked to provide consultation to the center's director for the first time. However, the other consultants still continued to be excluded from what they considered to be their advisory functions.

In April, 1966, the consultants held a meeting to discuss the future of their relationship with the corporation. The great majority concluded that the corporation regarded its relationship with the university as essential for public relations purposes only (and perhaps also required by its contract with OEO), and that it would probably continue to ignore the consultants' efforts to implement their advisory functions on policy issues. The underlying problem, they agreed, was the difference between the two institutions on fundamental concepts of the center's operation.

The consultants concluded that the gap between themselves and the corporation was too great to be bridged. By a vote of 16 to 0 (with 2 abstentions) they recommended to the university that it not seek to renew its contract with the corporation at its expiration on July 1, 1966. The university accepted this recommendation, and relations between the two institutions were discontinued on that date.

CONSEQUENCES

Before following the university's decision to terminate its relations with the Job Corps center, the corporation recruited consultants on an individual basis from other universities and from a private consulting firm. It made no efforts to enter into another contract with a university and hired its new consultants as individuals. These consultants had a view of their role different from that of the university group. They saw themselves as advisers to the corporation on such problems as the corporation would present to them, without intruding in the policy-making process. If they were asked, for example, what time the dormi-tory lights should be turned off, they would, after study, recommend a specific time.

QUESTIONS FOR DISCUSSION

1. What are the different roles of consultants illustrated in this case?

2. Should the university have entered into a subcontract which limited their freedom to make information public?

3. Did the corporation place inappropriate restrictions upon the university consultants?

4. Were the university consultants justified in ignoring the corporation's directive forbidding the release of information without prior corporation approval?

5. What could have been done differently by the corporation and the university during planning or operation which might have resulted in a more productive relationship?

A Service-Oriented Youth-Work Program Converts to Controlled Research

After several years of operation the administrators of a comprehensive youth-work agency decided to apply for federal funds to support con-version of its service-oriented program to a controlled research experi-ment. The research design was characterized by random assignment of youth to various service components of the program in an effort to determine their relative effectiveness in influencing subsequent expe-rience in the labor market.

Shortly after the agency announced its decision to conduct its future operations under a research design, some vocational counselors and other program staff members objected that the new commitment to research would in effect deny needed services to many trainees. Subsequently a variety of exceptions and a bypass of random assignment were established by the program administrators as a means of coping with these staff objections. While no formal decisions were made by the program operators to resolve the conflicting demands of research and service, service reemerged, after two years, as the program's basic operating principle through gradual and informal loosening of the research design's controls.

BACKGROUND

An experimental comprehensive youth-work program, conducted for several years with federal funds by a private agency in a large city, was faced with a decision about its future in early 1965. Its initial commitment had been to demonstrate new service techniques for aiding disadvantaged youth. Systematic evaluative research to test the effectiveness of these new techniques, however, was not emphasized under the original program. But with the expiration of its grant from a federal agency nearing, the agency's administration had to reach a decision on a future direction. Two alternatives seemed open: continued emphasis on services to disadvantaged youth, or shift to an explicit research orientation.

The agency's overall administration and the operators of its youth-work program considered the question, "Where do we go from here?" against a background of general staff satisfaction with the status quo —a positive sense of routine and commitment to service, with no major operational changes proposed. But the agency's administrators agreed in February, 1965, that a conversion of the youth-work program to a research orientation was necessary to preserve and enhance its "pioneering spirit" and national reputation in the youth-work field. The administrators believed that funds received under earlier contracts would probably be available only under such circumstances, although other sources might be approached for operating funds if the agency decided to maintain a service orientation.

The administration asked a member of its research staff to develop a specific proposal for a new research grant, and it was completed a month prior to the expiration of the previous grant in July, 1965. This design was intended to test such issues as the relative effects of concurrent educational services on job experiences of disadvantaged youth, the relative effects of systematic vocational evaluation before assignment, and the effectiveness of training programs conducted by the agency in its special work-crew program as contrasted with training to be provided outside the agency's service area with funds provided by another federal program.

The agency began to convert to operations under the new research design with a six-month pilot program beginning in July under temporary continuation grants. Federal funding of the new program was delayed and did not occur formally until December. Just before this funding deadline, pressure was generated by the federal agencies for several revisions of the proposal, and a last-minute meeting was held by six agency and program administrators to complete the design. At this meeting, a final form of the research design was agreed upon.

In essence, the design required random assignment of trainees to the various program components. A specified proportion, 48 per cent, of all trainees were thus to be assigned to outside training, and 52 per cent to the agency's work crews. Of these a certain proportion would then receive remedial educational services, while the rest would receive no such services; some trainees would undergo vocational evaluation before assignment to training, others not. The experiences of trainees would then be compared and some conclusions drawn about the relative effectiveness of the services they had received.

The program administrators accepted the final structure of the research design with little substantive discussion of possible operational problems among themselves or with members of the program staff. The decision-making group relied heavily on the authority of the researchers among them and became committed to this research design in the absence of any suitable alternatives. Some members of the group were enthusiastic about the proposal, believing that it would make a significant contribution to knowledge of youth-work programs and could influence national manpower policies. But others were skeptical about its potential effect on the agency's services to disadvantaged youth.

IDENTIFICATION OF THE PROBLEM

In July, 1965, a meeting was called to explain the new research design to the entire counseling staff, and to launch a six-month pilot period which would prepare them for transition to the controlled research experiment. Immediately after the need for random assignment of trainees became clear, a majority of the counselors and even some of their supervisors objected in private to its implications.

The counselors charged that the research design undermined the original approach and ideology of the agency, which in their view was intended to conduct an innovative, flexible, client-oriented program. Forcing the youngsters to accept arbitrary assignments seemed to most counselors to contradict the agency's expressed goal of individually designed service programs in which the trainees participated in the decision-making process. One counselor called the research design "test tubing the kids," and declared that this agency should not come to resemble those routinized agency-oriented programs which it had for so long publicly opposed.

When the staff sentiments became manifest, both the program and the research study directors were initially sympathetic. They told them a transition program was not easy but that in the long run the results of the research would permit this agency and others around the country to conduct even more effective service programs. They stressed some of the positive consequences of the program for service activities, such as permission to use certain federal funds for the agency's own work-crew program and new funds for a remedial educational component, and asserted that despite the priority of the research design over the agency's previous service orientation, the number of youngsters deriving work-training and supportive services would still be larger than that of any other youth-work agency in the city. In addition they pointed out that the research design provided a bypass for those youths the counselors considered ready for immediate job placement. Such youth would not be forced to undergo vocational training and therefore would become a part of the experiment.

These explanations did not satisfy some members of the counseling staff, who insisted among themselves that the experiment would not achieve its research objectives. Indeed many of them believed it was developed primarily to attract new federal research funds. In spite of these reservations the program administrators continued to implement the research design to which they had already committed the agency. The control focus of the agency's youth-work program was shifted from service to research, with the goal of gaining new knowledge of the relative effectiveness of various work-training and supportive services.

COPING WITH THE PROBLEM

It became apparent to the program supervisors as soon as the new design was made operational at the end of 1965 that many counselors had been convinced during the six-month pilot period that the research design did in fact deny needed service to some trainees. Many counselors continued to claim confusion about the goals of the research program and complained that they were unable to utilize their professional training. With major decisions affecting a trainee's assignment delegated to a table of random numbers, the counselors came to believe their training and skills had become superfluous.

Some of the counselors reacted by improvising ways to minimize the impact of random assignments on some trainees. For example, if a counselor knew, from a referral from another agency or from other trainees, that a client with certain vocational needs was coming to the agency on a given day, he might wait for the youngster outside the reception unit and ask him to step aside. The counselors would then determine when the number assigning the trainee to a specific service would come up and ask his trainee to come forward and receive it. By thus manipulating the sequence of the assignments, a counselor could overcome the arbitrary research design and match his trainees to needed services in a highly informal "counseling" fashion.

Another technique utilized by counselors when confronted with what they considered to be an unsound research design was to request, through their supervisors, exceptions for certain trainees. In addition to the bypass provided by the research design for youngsters considered ready for immediate job placement (many of these were Negro high-school graduates), counselors soon found groups whose special vocational problems had not been anticipated. How could they deal with a pregnant girl whose random assignment was to outside training which would require travel and work in an unknown and perhaps unfriendly environment? What should they do about the growing numbers of non-English-speaking trainees who were coming into the program and for whom almost no suitable outside positions were available?

Many requests for exceptions were made by counselors, and most were accepted by the study director. The study director tried to generalize these exceptions in an effort to minimize the number of individual counselor requests and to remedy some of the more obvious defects of the original research design. Pregnant girls, for example, were eliminated from outside work assignments, and non-English-speaking youngsters were given special language training before entering the research program. Also, since outside training positions did not become available until well after the research design became operational, attempts were made to place youngsters who should have been assigned to regular jobs by the research design.

But by the end of the first six months of pilot operation, the number of these exceptions had grown so large that the continued functioning of the research design was threatened. The study director had made so many exceptions that many of the research design categories, especially the outside positions and remedial education, were not being filled. Furthermore, a fairly sizable group of hard-core youngsters (those with special physical, behavioral, and other problems who the counselors believed were unsuited for entry into the regular service programs of the agency) had accumulated on counselor caseloads but did not appear in research statistics.

At this point the program director decided that the controlled research experiment was endangered by the inadequate number of trainees actually entering some components of the program. The study director (who occupied a position in the research organizational structure and was therefore not subordinate to the service, or program, director) was less concerned than the program director with conforming to the original design and proposed that it be modified. (The program director had final responsibility under the contract for fulfilling the terms of the grant proposal, while the research study director was responsible for analyzing the data delivered by the program.) But in addition, the research study director began to suspect that the original research design was adversely affecting the quality of services the program was providing the disadvantaged youth in the target population. When the study director, after having been demoted by the program director for alleged inability to supervise the research, became convinced the design would not be formally modified by permitting mere exceptions, he left the program and was replaced by the research director of the agency.

By this time it had become clear to the administrators of the agency that neither service nor research was being conducted adequately. Morale among both trainees and counselors declined sharply, and the dropout rate among the youth appeared to increase. Because he was contractually responsible for the program as well as the research, the program director played an increasingly active role in the conduct of research. In an effort to tighten up the operations, he established a monthly reporting system for each counselor's work load and called on those with a high rate of exceptions to explain them. Many counselors began to complain that they were being blamed for the high dropout rate and the failure of the program to deliver the required number of trainees to each category of the research design. Some trainees themselves complained about being "underpaid and overtested."

Under the research design the problem of unfilled positions was especially acute for dispersed training. Few trainees or counselors thought highly of the opportunities then available in the outside program; both agreed that the agency work crew was "good" and the outside program was "bad." Since a major goal of the research program was to compare the experiences of trainees in the two training programs, the attempted avoidance of one program component by trainees and counselors was a serious threat to the fulfillment of the research design. The program director therefore asked for a special report on the number of trainees "exempted" from outside training and the reasons for their exemption. In almost every case it was found that the reasons were good ones, viewed from a "service orientation."

By the summer of 1966 it was reported that the composition of the agency's clients was changing to include a much higher proportion of non-English-speaking youngsters and a higher proportion of females. General difficulty in recruiting adequate numbers of new trainees was identified by program staff as another major problem. The agency administrators did not want to conclude that the research design was itself responsible for these developments, and other explanations were sought. A tightening labor market, for example, was seen as providing more regular job opportunities for disadvantaged youth than were available a year before, and consequently fewer sought the assistance of the agency.

The need for more trainees in several components of the research program continued to be serious. New recruiting drives led to an increase in enrollees, but they were mostly non-English-speaking youth who needed special English-language education before assignment to the training program. The failure of arbitrary placement to provide sufficient numbers for certain components of the design became so critical that the proportion of intake randomly assigned to outside training by the research design was raised from 48 per cent to 60 per cent for several months.

In the fall of 1966 the agency and the federal department funding the program held an informal meeting to consider whether to attempt to maintain rigorous application of the research design. The participants agreed that the controls of the research design could be loosened on an informal basis, that changes in the numerical requirements could be made, and in general that service could resume its predominant place as a goal of the agency. While the research design could continue, it would be applied in a more flexible way.

CONSEQUENCES

By the middle of 1967, after two years of operation under a research design, the agency's youth-work program was moving back to a "service orientation," although still operating under the research design. Improvements had been made in the outside program, and trainees had found it more attractive. There had been turnover among the counseling staff, and the present counseling staff tended to be less professionally oriented (and thus perhaps more amenable to a program using random assignment techniques).

The research design, though never formally modified, had obviously been loosened as exceptions were established; the proportions of trainees in the various components were shifted in response to the problem of filling them; and the arbitrariness of actual assignment was reduced in view of some counselors' manipulation of the numerical sequence. The gradual and informal modification of the original design also provided for the assignment of *all* non-English-speaking trainees to a special education program and education for *all* clerical trainees regardless of the random numerical assignments.

QUESTIONS FOR DISCUSSION

1. Do you believe this youth-work agency, whose service program had been considered successful, should have embarked on this controlled research experiment?

2. Is there any way the counseling staff's resistance to the research program could have been overcome and the likelihood of their manipulating the design reduced?

3. Under what conditions can a controlled research experiment successfully be integrated with an ongoing service-oriented program?

4. What do you think were the consequences, both positive and negative, of the research program on the agency? The counseling staff? The trainees?

5. Explain the apparent reversal of roles between the program director and the study director concerning their attitudes toward rigorous adherence to the research design.

6. In light of the modifications, are useful research findings still possible?

Recalcitrant Service Agencies Force Change in a Research Design

卐卐

A university research group designed a study of potential and actual Neighborhood Youth Corps trainees. This study required access to the youths at their point of initial contact with the program in intake centers operated by various agencies, and was to follow their progress through the entire process of application, enrollment, assignment, and eventual completion of the program. The researchers did not anticipate any opposition by these agencies, but it became clear after the project began that several of them would be extremely reluctant to permit an outside group to interfere with their delivery of services to their clients.

After prolonged negotiations, the researchers succeeded in obtaining access to some intake centers, but failed with others. Since these recalcitrant agencies served a significant portion of the NYC trainees the project was designed to study, the researchers were forced to modify the original design.

BACKGROUND

In the spring of 1965 a university research group in a large city contracted with the Office of Economic Opportunity to conduct a long-term evaluation of Neighborhood Youth Corps trainees. The purpose of the study was to provide comprehensive information to NYC program planners and operators on the work attitudes and performance of Negro NYC trainees in the city, and to measure changes in these characteristics after the trainees' initial contact with the program.

More specifically, the study design provided for interviewing a group of 1,600 Negro youth about their motivations, expectations, and personal characteristics at the time of their first encounters with a job intake center. Their subsequent experience and performance in the NYC program and later in regular employment would then be compared with the baseline data. The researchers believed the study findings might serve to modify and strengthen the intake, counseling, and assignment procedures of the NYC as well as its placement and other program activities.

Carrying out the research design depended on securing access to the specified number of applicants at intake centers, which were operated by several anti-poverty organizations and their delegate agencies. Although the research group had no contact with these operating agencies prior to submitting its research proposal to the OEO, its planners were confident that access to the trainees served by the four or six agencies would not constitute a major problem and that negotiations for their cooperation could be carried out successfully after funds had been received and a research staff employed.

The intake centers to which the researchers needed access were located in the city's ghetto areas and were selected by the research group because of their access to the desired target population and their anticipated high intake rate of NYC trainees. They were operated by two private community anti-poverty agencies, a national social welfare organization operating as a delegate agency, and three intake centers of a municipally supported agency.

IDENTIFICATION OF THE PROBLEM

After the research was funded and a staff hired, the group met with the directors of the selected intake centers for the first time and broadly informed them of the purpose of the research. The researchers explained the need for the directors' cooperation in providing access to potential NYC trainees at their intake centers.

The initial response from the centers was cautious. They emphasized that their first commitment was to service, not research, and therefore that their first obligation was to serve their target population. They immediately began to question whether the research design might conflict with the delivery of their services. Would the trainees be alienated by the type of questions or the manner of the interview? Would the length of time required for the interviews bore the trainees and produce hostility toward the center?

After the researchers had assured one of the major agencies that, to the best of their knowledge, the research design would not conflict with their provision of services, permission was granted to station university interviewers at its intake center. But another key agency, then undergoing severe internal conflicts, deferred a decision and, in the view of the researchers, consciously avoided further dealings with them. Letters went unanswered, phone calls were not returned, and the researchers became convinced its directors felt threatened by outsiders studying its operations.

Since the existing research design was dependent for its success on cooperation from that intake center, the researchers were faced with the alternatives of continuing efforts to gain access to the recalcitrant agency, finding substitute cooperative agencies that met the needs of the study, or modifying their original research design to reflect their failure to reach a significant portion of the target population.

COPING WITH THE PROBLEM

Because modification of the research design was clearly the most drastic and least desirable alternative, the researchers decided to make additional efforts to win the cooperation of the agency. Informal contact was made with its research director, who advised that his personal intervention with the agency's director, together with a letter from the dean of the school of which the research group was a part, might influence a favorable decision. But he later informed the researchers that the agency director was preoccupied with the internal crisis and would refer any decision on cooperation with the research design to his board of directors. At this point more than three months had elapsed since the researcher's initial meeting with the agency.

Finally the agency board decided not to object to the researchers access to potential NYC trainees at its intake centers. But it granted the right of final decision to the program operators at the three intake centers under its control, one operated directly by the agency and two by its delegate agencies. The agency's director of work programs, after being informed of the board's decision, told the researchers that he would permit access to the trainees at the intake center operated directly by the agency, but that he could not control decisions by the delegate agencies which operated the other two centers under subcontract.

The university staff then met with the directors of the three centers. One, as previously directed, was prepared to move directly into arranging procedures for interviewing the job applicants. But the two delegate agencies expressed serious reservations about the entire project. One delegate agency, a national social welfare organization, stated that the proposed research would disrupt its intake processing, which was geared to the greatest possible speed in providing service to the clients. The director of its intake center further declared that the proposed research questionnaire asked for personal information that the applicants, already "anti-white," would resent. He also wished to know how the resulting data would be used, by whom they would be evaluated, and suggested that they be turned over to him before release. The other recalcitrant agency indicated similar reservations.

The researchers believed that some interagency distrust was another reason for the hostility of the two program operators to the request. The delegate agencies had been selected to operate the intake centers primarily for political reasons in an effort to give all established groups in the area "a share in the action," and relations between them and the agency serving as prime contractor were strained. The researchers suspected that the delegate agencies viewed the university as a spy for the prime contractor, to whom they would report on the effectiveness of the intake center's performance.

Since one of the delegate agencies had a small intake load, the researchers did not make further effort to gain access to its applicants. But appeals were made to the national office of the social welfare organization because its cooperation was especially crucial for the success of the original design. Its service area included a ghetto whose characteristics the researchers believed might differ significantly from those of other ghettos in the city.

The research instruments were fully explained, and offers to permit the intake center to control the time, location, and length of the interviews were made. But by late summer of 1965 the research group concluded that this agency would not cooperate under any conditions because it feared that shortcomings in its intake and referral procedures would be subject to outside scrutiny. The group therefore ended their efforts to persuade the agency to cooperate when, although never formally rejecting access to its trainees, it permitted a deadline for a final reply to the request for permission to pass.

After the loss of the large number of potential NYC trainees through the failure of the agency to cooperate with the research project, the only alternative remaining to the researchers was modification of the original design. By that time, six months after the study began, the number of NYC trainees passing through the intake centers had been determined with some accuracy, and the loss of the social welfare organization's intake center trainees was a great disappointment.

The original design was to follow a panel from initial application through enrollment and termination, and to follow those applicants who dropped out of the process before being assigned to the NYC. But the refusal to cooperate on the part of several intake centers meant that too few panelists would find their way into the NYC from the intake centers accessible to the research group. Consequently the research design was modified to include two panels instead of one. The first traced those applicants available at the intake centers who cooperated from application up to the point of their being assigned, if they were assigned, or up to three months after their application, whichever occurred first. The second panel group was selected from the enrollment forms of the Neighborhood Youth Corps payrolls, (available at the city welfare department, the central processing point for NYC paychecks) and followed them through to their various outcomes, including early termination, successful completion of assignment, etc.

The researchers regarded the establishment of two different panels as a significant deviation from the original research design because their findings could now no longer reflect the attitudes and motiva-

tions of all trainees prior to their first contact with the NYC program
—which had been a major initial goal of the study. But they were
forced to make this decision in the absence of any alternative method
of securing at the intake centers the required number of trainees for
the study.

The researchers finally succeeded in interviewing 700 youths at the
two intake centers to which they gained admittance, and were able to
include 700 NYC enrollees in the second panel—a total of 1,400 for
the whole project.

No difficulties were encountered in obtaining access to the NYC
payroll records, nor in interviewing either the applicants at the intake
centers or the trainees who had received work assignments at their job
sites.

CONSEQUENCES

Modification of the research design to include two separate panels
of youth had at least one positive consequence: the procedures of the
study were greatly accelerated. The new design permitted the researchers to interview a larger number of youth in a shorter period of
time than would have been possible if they had to rely solely on the
small flow of youth coming into the centers. This number could now
be greatly expanded by the additional names from the payroll records.

The major negative consequence of the operating agency's failure
to permit access to the researchers is that the results of the study will
not measure the changes in trainees' attitudes toward work or in self-
esteem that occurred between their first contact with the NYC program and subsequent stages of the program. The results will permit
measurement of changes that occurred between a point about three
months after the first contact and subsequently, but the original baseline has been lost.

QUESTIONS FOR DISCUSSION

1. What are the advantages and disadvantages in having a proposal for research on an action program developed by an outside research group with little direct connection to the action program?

2. Might the resistance of the recalcitrant agency have been overcome? If so, how?

3. Should the OEO have funded the research proposal without requiring guaranties of cooperation by intake centers?

4. How damaging to the original research goals has the design modification been?

5. To what extent is it feasible to develop a research design posed upon a program which has not begun operation?